Kauṭilīya Arthaśāstra Revisited

PHISPC MONOGRAPH SERIES ON HISTORY OF PHILOSOPHY, SCIENCE AND CULTURE IN INDIA

1. Science, Philosophy and Culture in Historical Perspective
   edited by D.P. CHATTOPADHYAYA AND RAVINDER KUMAR
2. Some Aspects of India's Philosophical and Scientific Heritage
   edited by D.P. CHATTOPADHYAYA AND RAVINDER KUMAR
3. Mathematics, Astronomy and Biology in Indian Tradition: Some Conceptual Preliminaries
   edited by D.P. CHATTOPADHYAYA AND RAVINDER KUMAR
4. Language, Logic and Science in India: Some Conceptual and Historical Perspectives
   edited by D.P. CHATTOPADHYAYA AND RAVINDER KUMAR
5. Primal Spirituality of the Vedas: Its Renewal and Renaissance
   by R. BALASUBRAMANIAN
6. Interdisciplinary Studies in Science, Technology, Philosophy and Culture
   by D.P. CHATTOPADHYAYA
7. Ancient Yoga and Modern Science
   by T.R. ANANTHARAMAN
8. Prolegomena to Any Future Historiography of Cultures and Civilizations
   by DAYA KRISHNA
9. Science and Spirituality: A Quantum Integration
   by AMIT GOSWAMI WITH MAGGIE GOSWAMI
10. On Rational Historiography
    by V. SHEKHAWAT
11. *Kauṭilīya Arthaśāstra* Revisited
    by SURENDRA NATH MITAL

11

Kauṭilīya Arthaśāstra Revisited

SURENDRA NATH MITAL

Project of History of Indian Science, Philosophy and Culture

CENTRE FOR STUDIES IN CIVILIZATIONS

First published in 2000
Reprinted in 2004
by Professor Bhuvan Chandel, Member Secretary
for Centre for Studies in Civilizations
36 Tughlakabad Institutional Area, Tughlakabad,
New Delhi-110 062

Distributed by
Munshiram Manoharlal Publishers Pvt. Ltd.
54 Rani Jhansi Road, New Delhi-110 055

ISBN : 81-87586-03-6

Typeset by Centre for Studies in Civilizations, New Delhi-110 048
printed at Durga Print-O-Graph, F-262-C, Pandav Nagar,
Delhi-110091

Contents

Foreword

The traditional fabric of the body politic in Indian Civilizations has been woven through the co-operation of three different strands namely, the Sage, the Ruler and the People. The Sages, Seers and Thinkers provided guidance and training to the Rulers. The whole tradition of *Arthaśāstra* was created in this process. The most celebrated figure in the Indian political tradition has been undoubtedly that of Kauṭilya who composed his justly famous *Arthaśāstra*, for the guidance of Candragupta Maurya. This image of Kauṭilya and Candragupta working together to build a vast empire, is one of the lasting memories of Indian political history. Unfortunately, the *Arthaśāstra* was lost for a long time and when it was discovered, western scholars subjected it to very unsympathetic criticism. It was opined that the whole story of Kauṭilya in relation to Candragupta Maurya is without any historical basis, that the *Arthaśāstra* now discovered is a late and inauthentic patch-work. This hostile criticism was sought to be rebutted by a number of eminent Indian scholars. However, special prestige continued to be attached to the opinions of those who were connected with the colonial rulers of India. The latest and the best known work in this connection is that of Trautmann's *Kauṭilya and the Arthaśāstra*. In this work it is attempted to distinguish the different sections of the texts with reference to their authorship on a stylometric basis with the help of statistical calculations through a computer. The highly technical nature of the arguments has inhibited a free and wide discussion on the views expressed by Trautmann and the mystique of the computer has given it undue prestige.

Dr Mital, the author of the present monograph, has put the world of Indological scholarship under his debt by carefully and exhaustively analyzing stylistic and statistical arguments of Trautmann and showing that he is guilty of grave errors and confusion. The way stylometric statistics has been used by Trautmann is faulty not only in arbitrarily classifying different sections of the text through the use of inconsistent stylometric criteria but also of arbitrary sampling. The whole work rests on a circular mode of argumentation.

The net result is that the antiquity and authenticity of Kauṭilya's *Arthaśāstra* remained unimpugned unless further facts were to be discovered contradictory to it.

Dr Mital has truly redeemed his *ṛṣi-ṛṇa* as a teacher and student of *Daṇḍanīti*. He deserves congratulations for his work which has been appreciated by specialists like Professor A.D. Pant. Professor D.P. Chattopadhyaya, the Director of the PHISPC and the Chairman of Centre for Studies in Civilizations, has been kind enough to agree to publish Dr Mital's monograph under the auspices of the Centre. All readers would be beholden to Professor Chattopadhyaya.

G.C. PANDE

Preface

This monograph consists of two articles written originally for different purposes; they are now combined to form two parts of it. The first article is on the 'Date of the *Arthaśāstra*'. There is nothing much in it that can claim any originality. Sir William Jones equated Sandrakottos of Greek writers with Candragupta Maurya and Max Müller, in his *History of Ancient Sanskrit Literature*, collected all the materials about Sandrakottos found in Greek writings and tried to show (though not very successfully) that it referred to Candragupta Maurya, who, on the ground that Megasthenes had come to his court as an ambassador of Selucas Nikator, was said to have ruled as Emperor of India in the fourth century BC. This is the reason why when the *Arthaśāstra* of Kauṭilya alias Cāṇakya alias Viṣṇugupta was discovered by Shri Sham Śastri at the beginning of this century, many scholars concluded that since the guru and guide of Candragupta Maurya was its author, it must have been composed in the fourth century BC. Some Western scholars did not like this inference as that would make Kauṭilya a contemporary of Plato and Aristotle. So while accepting the date of Candragupta Maurya as fixed by Sir William Jones and Max Müller, they challenged the date of the *Arthaśāstra*. This was done mainly by J. Jolly, A.B. Keith and M. Winternitz, further continued by O. Stein. However, this was not accepted by Indian scholars, and a host of them replied to the arguments of the above mentioned Western writers.

The first part of this monograph refers to the arguments put forward by Jolly, Keith and Winternitz and shows why they are not acceptable. Although there is little that is original in this part, the way the arguments of both sides are presented here is my own. I have also tried to refute some of the arguments by Western scholars, hitherto unchallenged. However, all these by themselves do not make the monograph worth much.

Professor B.N.S. Yadava had once suggested to me that I might examine the statistical theory of Thomas Trautmann. Professor G.C. Pande also emphasised that Trautmann's arguments needed to be refuted cogently. I felt that if Trautmann's thesis is to be examined, it cannot be done only on the basis of the statistics in his book. Therefore, I began to collect my own statistics about *ca* and *vā,* the only basis on which Trautmann's thesis is based. Though it involved a considerable amount of manual work (the writer did not have the facility of a computer), yet it helped me to clearly understand the reason for the differing use of *ca* and *vā* in different parts of the *Arthaśāstra.* I have tried to put forward that reason here in this monograph. How much of what I say is correct is left to the scholarly readers to judge.

In the *Journal of American Oriental Society* (1972, pp. 498–500), Trautmann's *Kauṭilya and the Arthaśāstra* was reviewed by Ludwig Sternbach of the University of Sorbonne, Paris, in which he suggested that *Kauṭilya's Arthaśāstra* contains many peculiarities of language. 'If these...would have been analysed, the statistical method probably would have borne better results than the unimportant use of words *eva, ca* and *vā,* and the results would probably be quite different' (p. 499). He has quoted, from different Books of the *Arthaśāstra,* various examples of these peculiarities of language to show that it is the work of one and not of different authors. Sternbach says, 'the premise that the *Arthaśāstra* was a compilation containing the work of at least three hands is an attractive one and perhaps well taken, but the proof of it is nil'.

After going through the arguments advanced by Professor Sternbach for proving the unity, and, thus, the one-man authorship of the *Arthaśāstra*, the statistical analysis of this monograph should have been considered unnecessary. But even after this, it could be said that, though grammatically and semantically the *Arthaśāstra* could be demonstrated as having been written by one author, different Books in it are so distinguished from one another that it could lead its readers to conclude that it was composed by a number of authors. According to Trautmann, the difference in the use of *ca* (and) and *vā* (or) in different Books (*adhikaraṇas*) of the *Arthaśāstra* is one such ground. Trautmann has not pointed out any other precise reason. Though in his compound–length study he has pointed out some differences in the Books of the *Arthaśāstra*, these differences do not tally with those pointed out by him on the basis of his *ca-vā* study (see pp. 107–8 of this monograph). In any case, the statistics of *ca* and *vā* as collected by me show that the difference in the frequency of use of *ca* and *vā* is found not only in different Books of the *Arthaśāstra* but also in certain chapters of various Books when compared with certain other chapters of those very Books, and not only that; different parts of certain chapters reveal similar differences. A comparative study of all these proves that the difference in the use of these two indeclinables is due to the necessity of having to use either *ca* or *vā* according to the context. The necessity of using *ca* and *vā* according to contextual difference arose, as already pointed out, sometimes in two or more parts of certain chapters and sometimes in various chapters of different Books themselves. Once this fact is grasped, the view that there were several (three or four) authors who were responsible for this difference, can be justly set aside. It is mainly to present this conclusion that this monograph has been written.

I am deeply grateful to Professor G.C. Pande, Professor D.P. Chattopadhyaya, Professor A.D. Pant and Professor B.N.S. Yadava. I am indebted to Shri Dipen Mitra for reading the typescript with great care, and suggesting many linguistic and stylistic improvements, most of which were accepted by me, and to Dr Bhagat Oinam, who helped me immensely at every stage of the publication of the book particularly in the correction of references given at the end of each of the two parts and at a later stage to Shri Ishwar Singh also. I am not only grateful to Dr Anoop Chaturvedi for his chi-square tests done for me but also to Dr G.S. Pande of the same department for his help in other kind of statistical work. I thank Shri Partap Singh Sharma and Km. Indu Menon for typing and typesetting this manuscript.

SURENDRA NATH MITAL

New Delhi
July 10, 2000

PART I

Date of *Arthaśāstra*

The *Kauṭilīya Arthaśāstra* is the most important work on politics in ancient India. Though the *Śukranītisāra* is also an independent work and seems to be quite original, yet the *Kauṭilīya Arthaśāstra* has exercised a greater influence, and the *Kāmandakīya Nītisāra*, the *Nītivākyāmṛta* of Somadeva, the eighth *ucchvāsa* of the novel *Daśakumāracarita*, the *Pañcatantra* and the *Mudrārākṣasa* draw much or some of their material from the *Arthaśāstra*.

The time of the composition of the *Kauṭilīya Arthaśāstra* appears to be more or less certain. Kauṭilya was the guide and advisor of Candragupta Maurya. If Candragupta belongs to the fourth century BC, as the general history books say, on the ground of the identity of Sandrokottos of Greek writers with Candragupta Maurya, then Kauṭilya also lived in the fourth century BC. If the identity is doubted as has been by M. Toyer in his edition of the *Rājataraṅgiṇī*, then Candragupta Maurya and Kauṭilya might have lived earlier. In spite of the association of Candragupta Maurya and Kauṭilya, some of the Western writers have, while accepting the date and historicity of Candragupta Maurya, doubted the existence of Kauṭilya, or that he wrote the *Arthaśāstra*, and they have tried to place *Arthaśāstra* at a later date. Therefore, a discussion of the date of composition of the *Arthaśāstra* is necessary, and though this has been done by several Western and Indian scholars, the facts may be recapitulated, but in a different order.

1. Traditional Opinion

For determining the date of the *Arthaśāstra*, three questions must be considered. One is the relationship of Cāṇakya and Candragupta Maurya and of their overthrowing the Nandas. The second question is, if Cāṇakya and Viṣṇugupta and Kauṭilya were the same person, and the third, if Kauṭilya wrote a work on politics. If the answers to all the three questions are positive, then it follows that Kauṭilya or Cāṇakya or Viṣṇugupta, who installed Candragupta on the throne, wrote the *Arthaśāstra* at the time when Candragupta was ruling, i.e. in the fourth century BC, and that all these are facts which have been denied by some Western writers, while the Indian tradition accepts them to be true.

(a) Association of Cāṇakya and Candragupta

We may first consider the coming together of Cāṇakya and Candragupta. Here one finds that this tradition—their association—has been universally accepted in India. It has been, as in the *purāṇas,* briefly stated by the *Mahāvaṁśa* (Buddhist). The *Mahāvaṁśa* says that 'Brāhmaṇa Cāṇakya, after having killed, in fierce anger, the ninth (*Nanda*) Dhanananda, he anointed him, born in the dynasty of the Kṣatriya Mauryas (and) possessed of royal splendour, known as Candragupta, on the kingdom of the whole of Jambūdvīpa'.[1] An earlier work *Dīpavaṁśa* simply mentioned that Candragupta ruled for 24 years (similar to what the *purāṇas* say) and that his son was Bindusāra and Bindusāra's son was Priyadarśī.[2] The *purāṇas* also corroborate these facts as mentioned in *Dīpavaṁśa* and *Mahāvaṁśa,* though they name the Brāhmaṇa as Kauṭilya in place of Cāṇakya. The *Viṣṇu Purāṇa* says:[3] 'And then the Brāhmaṇa Kauṭilya shall exterminate these nine Nandas. After their annihilation the Mauryas shall enjoy the earth. Kauṭilya shall anoint Candragupta (born in the family of the Mauryas) on the kingdom. Also, his son shall be Bindusāra and then also his son Aśokavardhana.' All this is found with minor differences in four other *purāṇas* (in verse).[4] The fact of the co-operation of Cāṇakya and Candragupta is also found in the tales in the *Mahāvaṁśa Ṭīkā* and some Jaina canonical works. The story related there is that Cāṇakya felt insulted at the court of the Nanda king, and then he vowed that he would destroy the Nandas. He took a boy Candragupta as his protégé. They together invaded Pāṭaliputra but were at first defeated. After learning that it was their weakness to have invaded the capital directly without subduing the outer areas, they attacked the place again and Candragupta was anointed king by Cāṇakya.

In political literature itself Kāmandaka in his *Nītisāra* refers to Kauṭilya as having destroyed the Nandas in order to place Candragupta on the throne.[5] He salutes Viṣṇugupta and speaking about him says[6]: 'Through whose magic spells, (of one) with lustre glowing like the thunderbolt, was destroyed together with his very roots (i.e. with his *dravyaprakṛtis*—ministers, army, treasury, etc., or, never to rise again) the mountain-like Nanda, full of majesty, who performed sacrifices on all religious festivals. Who alone (i.e. without the help of the army and without any treasury) through his wise counsel and valour like that of Skanda (the commander-in-chief of the gods) snatched the earth for the moon among men—Candragupta.' The commentators here suggest that he had two powers, *mantraśakti* or wise counsel and *utsāhaśakti* or valour, but did not have the third power—the *prabhuśakti,* army and treasury.

Not only in the political literature (in Kāmandaka apart from the *Kauṭilīya,* which shall be referred to below) and not only in the religious and historical works (the *purāṇas* are religious books with a historical tinge and it is in their historical portion, which has been ordinarily accepted and used by Western scholars, particularly the portion concerning the *Kaliyuga* era where reference to Kauṭilya and Candragupta is found) has the event relating to the ousting of Nandas been given, but also in political fiction (*Mudrārākṣasa*) and in other literature there is mention of these two. In *Kathāsaritsāgara*[7] (which says that it closely follows the *Bṛhatkathā* of Gunāḍhya, as also in the *Bṛhatkathāmañjarī*) also is found the story of Cāṇakya. Cāṇakya felt insulted by the behaviour of King Yogānanda for ousting him from a ceremony conducted at the palace and he (Cāṇakya) decided to kill the king. Having carried out his intention he installed Candragupta on the throne. There is much fictitious element in the story as is usually found in works of historical fiction. In spite of all that, the attempt made by Cāṇakya to dislodge the Nandas from the throne and the installation of Candragupta as the king is the keynote of the story.

The tale of *Mudrārākṣasa* starts after Candragupta is placed on the throne by Cāṇakya, and the latter is manipulating to gain the support of Rākṣasa, a very sincere minister of the Nandas, for Candragupta. On the other hand, at the urging of Rākṣasa, Parvataka's son, Malayaketu, tries to attack the forces of Candragupta. The allusion of making Candragupta the king after the destruction of the Nandas is found at the very beginning of the drama. The stage-manager, hearing a voice from the background (1.7) says: 'He is that (person of) crooked intellect (*kuṭilamati* i.e. otherwise Kauṭilya), who has forcibly burnt (destroyed) the Nanda dynasty in the fire of his anger, and who, on hearing of the lunar eclipse (*candragrahaṇa*), because of the similarity of words, is thinking that some enemy is attacking the Maurya Candra (moon)'. Later on (after 1.13) Cāṇakya himself says, 'Without having caught (brought under control) Rākṣasa, how (can it be said) that I have dug up the Nanda dynasty, or that I have made the royal power (*lakṣmī*) permanent for Candragupta?'

Thus the play clearly refers to the association of Cāṇakya and Candragupta. The novel *Daśakumāracarita* also hints at this fact where, in the eighth *ucchvāsa*, Vīrabhadra, at the beginning of his address to King Anantavarman, says that *daṇḍanīti* has been summarized by Viṣṇugupta (the name given by Cāṇakya to himself at the end of the *Arthaśāstra*) for the Maurya (Candragupta).

Whether we take religious or historical literature, or political literature or literary works or the Buddhist or Jaina works in ancient India, we find that it was universally accepted that Cāṇakya, together with his disciple or protégé Candragupta destroyed the Nandas and Candragupta was placed on the throne. To deny one part of this tradition (about Cāṇakya) would be to deny the other part also, for the tradition rests wholly on the fusion of the two parts. To refuse to give credibility to this tradition would be to turn a blind eye to one of the most important facts of ancient Indian history.

(b) Cāṇakya, Viṣṇugupta and Kauṭilya—synonymity of names

The second point to be discussed is the identity of Cāṇakya with Viṣṇugupta and Kauṭilya. At the beginning of this examination it should be made clear that wherever there is any mention of the ousting of the Nandas and/or of the installing of Candragupta on the throne, that should be understood to be a reference to Cāṇakya, and where the writing of a work (*Arthaśāstra*) is spoken of that refers to Kauṭilya whether the name Cāṇakya or Kautilya is specifically mentioned or not. Thus, when *Daśakumāracarita* mentions Viṣṇugupta's work on *Daṇḍanīti*, the reference is to Kauṭilya and it is widely accepted to be so, or the mention of Kauṭilya in the *purāṇas* in connection with the Nandas and Mauryas refers to Cāṇakya, because at most of the places where there is a mention of the overthrowing of the Nandas, it is Cāṇakya who is said to have done that, whereas the *Arthaśāstra* is widely known to have been written by Kauṭilya or as the *Kauṭilīya Arthaśāstra* (even in the *Arthaśāstra* itself).

While dealing with the synonymity of the three names, it would be better to start with the Buddhist and Jaina literature and the *purāṇas*. In the Buddhist and Jaina works, it is Cāṇakya who is said to have dethroned the Nandas and crowned Candragupta instead. Whereas, when the *purāṇas* refer to the same incident, they speak of Kauṭilya as having done so. This means that the same individual is known as Cāṇakya as well as Kauṭilya.

Among literary works, in *Mudrārākṣasa* Cāṇakya is specifically equated with Viṣṇugupta as also with Kauṭilya. The play ordinarily names the hero (or the main character of the play) as Cāṇakya, but Cāṇakya while saluting Rākṣasa calls himself Viṣṇugupta.[8] So also Malayaketu calls him Viṣṇugupta.[9] Again, in the first Act of the play, Cāṇakya calls himself Viṣṇugupta, when he warns the *śreṣṭhin* Candanadāsa, a friend of Rākṣasa, that Rākṣasa cannot destroy Candragupta just as (he himself) Viṣṇugupta has destroyed the Nandas.[10] Therefore, according to the play, Cāṇakya and Viṣṇugupta are the same person. When we consider the third name of Cāṇakya, i.e. Kauṭilya, Rākṣasa, depicting the character of Cāṇakya, calls him Kauṭilya (*Kuṭilāṃ Kauṭilyasya pracintayato matiṃ*) and so does also the stage manager (*sūtradhāra*), at the beginning while introducing the play, calling Cāṇakya as *Kuṭilamati* (a pun on the name Kauṭilya).

In Daṇḍin's *Daśakumāracarita* (II.8), it is said: 'This (*daṇḍanīti*) has been summarized by Viṣṇugupta,' thus equating Viṣṇugupta with Kauṭilya. The work refers to Cāṇakya in this very *ucchvāsa* in two places. In one place it makes the swindler Vihārabhadra say, 'They (*adhyākṣas*), through their intelligence make the forty ways of embezzlement (*haraṇopāya*), pointed out by Cāṇakya, a thousand-fold'.[11] At another place it makes the honest minister (Vasurakṣita) deplore the trait of his king (Anantavarman of Videha) in the words: 'Cāṇakya has truly said, "Harmful persons who follow the known inclinations (of the king) become favourites". (But) even competent people, cast out (i.e. away) from those inclinations become disliked'.[12] Here, whereas the *Arthaśāstra* is referred to at both places, the name of the quoted authority is given as Cāṇakya, making the two the same person. Thus in these three references Viṣṇugupta and Kauṭilya and Cāṇakya have been equated. In the eighth *ucchvāsa* itself the daily time-table of the king is divided into those sixteen parts of day and night and in exactly the same manner as has been done by Kauṭilya (I.19. 9-24). So it has to be quoted in full with the work of each division of the day in the two works given side by side.

(1) *Kauṭilya—pūrvedivasasyaṣṭabhāge. . . āyavyayau ca śṛṇuyāt; Daśakumāracarita—āyavyayajātamahnaḥ prathame aṣṭame bhāge śrotavyam.*

(2) *Kauṭ.—Dvitīye paurjānapadānāṃ kāryāṇi paśyet; Daśa—Dvitīye'nyonyaṃ vivadamānānāṃ janānāmākrośādahyamānakarṇaḥ.*

(3) *Kauṭ.—Tritīye snānabhojanaṃ seveta; Daśa—Tritīye snātuṃ bhoktuṃ ca labhate.*

(4) *Kauṭ.—Caturthe hiraṇyapratigrahaṃ; Daśa—Caturthe hiraṇyapratigrahāya.*

(5) *Kauṭ.—Pañcame mantripariṣadā . . . mantrayeta; Daśa—Pañcame mantracintayā . . .*

(6) *Kauṭ.—Ṣaṣṭhe svairavihāraṃ mantraṃ vā seveta; Daśa—Ṣaṣṭhe svairavihāro mantro vā sevyaḥ;*

(7) *Kauṭ.—Samptame hastyaśvarathāyudhīyān paśyet; Daśa—Saptame caturaṅgabalapratyavekṣaṇaprayāśaḥ.*

(8) *Kauṭ.—Aṣṭame senāpatisakho vikramaṃ cintayeta pratiṣṭhite'hani sandhyāmupāsīta; Daśa—Aṣṭame'sya senāpatisakhasya vikramacintākleśaḥ, punarupāśyaiva sandhyāṃ.*

(9) *Kauṭ.—Prathame rātribhāge gūḍhapuruṣān paśyet; Daśa—Prathame rātribhāge guḍhapuruṣā dṛṣṭavyāḥ.*

(10) *Kauṭ.—Dvitīye snānabhojanaṃ kurvīta svādhyāyaṃ ca; Daśa—Dvitīye bhojanāntaraṃ śrotriyā iva svādhyāyamārabheta.*

(11–13) *Kauṭ.—Tritīyetūryaghoṣeṇa saṁviṣṭaścaturthapañcamau śayīta; Daśa—tritīye tūryaghoṣeṇa saṁviṣṭaścaturthapañcamau śayīta.*

(14) *Kauṭ.—Ṣaṣṭhe. . . śāstramitikartavyatāṃ ca cintayet; Daśa—Punaḥ ṣaṣṭhe sāstracintākāryacintārambhaḥ.*

(15) *Kauṭ.—Saptame mantramadhyāsīta; Daśa—Saptame tu mantragraho.*

(16) *Kauṭ.—Aṣṭame ṛtvigācārya-purohitasvastyanāni pratigrahṇīyāt . . . ; Daśa—Aṣṭame purohitādayo'bhetya . . . kṛtamebhiḥ svastyayanaṃ kalyāṇataraṃ bhavati.*

It will be seen how close the similarity is and that *Daśakumāracarita* has nearly quoted Kauṭilya's *Arthaśāstra*. What is clear from all this is that Daṇḍin equates Viṣṇugupta with Cāṇakya specifically, and both these names also with Kauṭilya, the writer of the present *Arthaśāstra*, inferentially.

In the introductory chapter of the *Pañcatantra* it is said that the king Amaraśakti expresses his desire that his sons should become learned and one of his ministers says that for this they shall have to study the *Dharmaśāstras* of Manu and others, the *Arthaśāstras of* Cāṇakya and others and the *Kāmaśāstras* of Vātsyāyana and others (between the 8th and the 9th verse). At the very beginning of *Pañcatantra* (2nd verse) the writer Viṣṇuśarmā bows to five writers of Politics (*nayaśāstra*), viz. Vācaspati, Śukra, Parāśara, his son (Vyāsa) and Cāṇakya. In the 47th verse of the Book II (*tantra*) three kinds of policies are mentioned—those recommended by Viṣṇugupta, Bhārgava (Śukra) and Bṛhaspati respectively. Thus, at all these three places the writer uses Cāṇakya and Viṣṇugupta as synonyms for Kauṭilya.

Similarly, when Kāmandaka speaks of Viṣṇugupta as having snatched the earth from the Nandas for the moon among men Candragupta, and, as having brought out the nectar of *nītiśāstra* from out of the ocean of *Arthaśāstra* works, he first identifies Viṣṇugupta with Cāṇakya and then with Kauṭilya.

The reason for a single individual being known as Viṣṇugupta or Cāṇakya must also be understood. He is known as Cāṇakya because, according to Yādavaprakāśa's *Vaijayantī,* he is *Caṇakātmajaḥ* (either the son of Caṇaka or a person born in Caṇaka's birthplace). He is called Viṣṇugupta because it is the name given to him at the time of *saṁskāra* (christening ceremony—*Jayamaṅgalāṭikā* on Kāmandaka I.6). There are two explanations for the person being called Kauṭilya. The commentary *Jayamaṅgalā* on the *Kāmandakīya Nītisāra* says that it is a *gotra* name (on I.6), whereas the commentary *Upādhyāyanirpekṣā* (on 1.2), explaining the word *apratigrāhakāṇāṃ,* derives the work *kuṭila* from *kuṭi,* i.e. an earthen pitcher (*kutirghaṭa ucyate).* Therefore, *kuṭila* means those who in the morning gather as much grain as is necessary for *homa* or for five great *yajñas* and not more, and thus are known as *kumbhīdhānyakas.*

Born in such a family he is known as Kauṭilya. (*Ṛṣiṇāmivā-pratigrāhakāṇāṃ yathā ṛṣyaḥ apratigrāhakā nirdvandvāt, tathā ete gārhasthyadharmamanupālyanto'pi apratigrāhakāḥ. Kuṭilatvāt kuṭirghaṭa ucyate. Taṃ dhānyabhṛtam lānti saṁgrahaṇanti prātaḥsamaye homādyarthaṃ nādhikaṃ, adhikaṃ tu brāhamaṇānuddiśya sadyaḥ prakṣālayanti iti kuṭilāḥ kumbhīdhānyā iti prasiddhāḥ. Ataeva Kuṭilānāma-patyaṃ Viṣṇuguptaḥ Kauṭilya ityuktaḥ*).

(c) Kauṭilya: Writer of the *Arthaśāstra*

That Kauṭilya or Viṣṇugupta or Cāṇakya is the writer of the *Arthaśāstra* (the third point) must be clear from what has been said above, that is, from Kāmandaka's statement that Viṣṇugupta 'brought out the nectar of *Nītiśāstra* from the ocean of *Arthaśāstra* works', from the position of the *Daśakumāracarita* that 'this (*daṇḍanīti*) has been summarized by Viṣṇugupta in 6000 *ślokas* (the number of *ślokas*, as having been referred to by Kauṭilya in his *Arthaśāstra* I.1.18) for the Maurya king', and from *Pañcatantra's* mentioning that Cāṇakya or Viṣṇugupta is the writer of *Arthaśāstra*. Apart from this the *Tantrākhyāyikā*, which according to Kane is not later than AD 300, bows to writers of political science (lit. the science of kingship) and includes Cāṇakya among them[13] (thus considering Cāṇakya and Kauṭilya to be the same person). The *Kādambarī* calls the *Kauṭilyaśāstra* cruel, for it contains wicked advice. Lastly, Utpala, the writer of a commentary on the *Yogayātrā* of Varāhamihira, quotes Cāṇakya's *Arthaśāstra*,[14] at least in three places.

(d) Evidence of the *Kauṭilīya Arthaśāstra*

In the end it would be useful to consider the evidence of the *Kauṭilīya Arthaśāstra* itself, which corroborates all the three above mentioned points. Let us take the relevant passages one by one and draw the necessary conclusions at the end.

(*i*) The very first *sūtra* of the *Arthaśāstra* says, 'This one treatise on politics has been written by bringing (the material) together (i.e. consulting and synthesizing the teachings of) all the *Arthaśāstras* written by the former teachers, for obtaining and nourishing this earth'. This claim, that he consulted all the previous works on the subject, could have been made by none other than the author himself.

(*ii*) Therefore, the verse at the end of the chapter should be interpreted accordingly, i.e. according to the first *sūtra* even though it has been done otherwise, that is, it has been considered spurious. 'The treatise, composed by Kauṭilya, (is) easy to learn and to comprehend, (is) definite with regard to its essence, meaning and matter, (and is) free from diffusion.'[15] Kangle thinks that 'the *śloka* I.1.19 does not seem to be original and was probably interpolated by some other hand'.[16] He also considers the preceding *sūtra,* i.e. I.1.18, which gives the extent of the work, i.e. 15 *adhikaraṇas,* 150 chapters, 180 *prakaraṇas* and 6000 *ślokas,* to be an interpolation.[17] He has two reasons for holding this opinion. Firstly, that 'the old Malayalam commentary (cb) does not contain *sūtra* 1.1.18, nor the *śloka* that follows'. Secondly, he doubts that the statement about the work containing 6000 *ślokas* stems from the author himself.[18] 'The present work is mainly in prose. How then are we to understand the statement about 6000 *ślokas?* One explanation would be that a *śloka* is to be understood as standing for a group of thirty-two syllables even if they be in prose.... Their number together with that of the real *ślokas* comes to about 5370 in the new edition.'[19] However, Kangle contradicts himself on both these counts. About the first argument, viz., that these two (the aphorism and the verse) are not found in the Malayalam commentary, Kangle adds, 'However, the earlier available manuscript that from Patan Bhandar (D) contains the passage indicating that it is fairly old'. So considering these two statements to be interpolations simply on the ground that it is not found in only one commentary, however old, though not older than the manuscript (D), is not sufficient proof of its being an interpolation. With respect to the number of *ślokas,* though the number of computed *ślokas* in Kangle's edition comes to 5370, if Kauṭilya mentions the number as roughly 6000, or, if, as Kangle demurringly suggests that 6000 *ślokas* can be understood to refer to *sūtras* in the text, there cannot be much objection to what Kauṭilya has said. In addition to this, Kangle adds that according to the *Daśakumāracarita* also the present work is abridged in 6000 *ślokas.* The rejection of the *sūtra* on the basis mainly of the mention of 6000 *ślokas* is wrong, particularly when the statement about *adhikaraṇas* (Books–15), *adhyāyas* (chapters–150) and *prakaraṇas* (sections–180) is found to be correct and its being considered an interpolation simply on that one ground does not appear to be justified.

(*iii*) At the end of the chapter which deals with the king's edicts (II.10), it is said, 'Having followed all the works on the subject,[20] and having perceived the practice of states, Kauṭilya has written of this method of issuing the edicts for the sake of the king'. (Translations of all words are based on Apte's Dictionary). The use of singular for the king shows that this has been written mainly for the sake of the king who ruled at the time of Kauṭilya, i.e. for Candragupta Maurya, and it is difficult to accept Kangle's translation of *'narendra'* in plural, or his contention that *'narendra'* is not used for Candragupta Maurya. Kane, of course, says[21] that *'narendārthe'* may have been purposely used in two senses: one, for the kings in general, and two, for the particular king, i.e. for Candragupta.

(*iv*) At the end (XV.1.73), in the last *śloka* of the last chapter it is said, 'This treatise has been composed by him who in anger quickly lifted up the science (from the low level it had fallen during the reign of the Nandas), and arms (to destroy the Nandas), and the earth that has gone to (fallen under the control of) the Nandas (from out of their hands)'.[22] Kangle considers this *śloka* also to be an interpolation. 'The same (i.e. like I.1.19) would also appear to be the case with the last *śloka* XV.1.73',[23] but as he seems to have given no reason for his own view here, it is difficult to accept that Kangle's opinion is correct. It is a sort of a concluding statement made by Kauṭilya or his synonym Cāṇakya.

(*v*) 'Having frequently observed mutual discrepancy of the commentators on the (various) treatises, Viṣṇugupta himself wrote both the *sūtras* and their commentaries.' Kangle considers this stanza, at the very end after the colophon to be clearly a later addition, because firstly, the stanza says that the treatise contains both the *sūtra* and the *bhāsya,* but the 'text contains only *sūtras* and no *bhāṣya*'[24] and secondly, because he uses his personal name' Viṣṇugupta in the verse, whereas at all other places in the book the *gotra* name Kauṭilya has been used. This raises doubts about the genuineness of the stanza. Trautmann adds two more reasons[25], that it is a metre otherwise unknown to the work (*āryā*) and that it follows the final colophon. Of course, the last ground that the śloka comes after the last colophon, can be taken as a good reason for considering that the *śloka* was a later addition. It is also true that there is no *bhāṣya* in the book in the sense that a *bhāṣya* 'takes every word in the *sūtra* and explains it fully', but it is a *bhāṣya* in the sense that there are 'enumerations followed by definitions and explanations', e.g. I.9.5-7 may be a *bhāṣya* on I.9.4 or I.10.2-13 can be a *bhāṣya* on I.10.1. Kauṭilya may have used the word *bhāṣya* in the sense that difficult or uncommon words have been explained in the sentences following them so that the possibility of mutual discrepancies in explaining these words could be avoided. The other reasons, that only the name Viṣṇugupta is used here or that the verse in the *āryā* metre is not found elsewhere, are not sound enough reasons for considering the verse as not genuine, because at the end Kauṭilya may have decided to give his personal name also, and the writers are free to use any metre as and where they like. Even the fact that the verse comes after the last colophon can be taken to be a good reason for considering the verse to be spurious only if it is not found in the manuscripts.

The conclusions that can be drawn from the above quotations from the *Arthaśāstra* of Kauṭilya are, firstly, that Kauṭilya is the writer of the *Arthaśāstra* (passages II and IV above), that it was he who was instrumental in destroying the Nandas (and by implication of having put Candragupta on the throne, i.e. of his association with Candragupta passages III and IV above) and that Viṣṇugupta and Kauṭilya are synonymous (and by implication Cāṇakya also—passages II, III, IV and V taken together). Therefore, because of all the above mentioned facts the *Arthaśāstra* must have been composed in the period when Candragupta Maurya was ruling in India, i.e. the 4th century BC, the presently accepted date of Candragupta. The scholars who want to place it in a later period have somehow tried to explain away the above supporting facts, and their views are taken up hereafter for consideration.

2. Views of Jolly, Keith and Winternitz

The conclusion that the *Kauṭilīya* was composed in the fourth century BC has been challenged by several scholars. This was first done by Jolly, who in 1914 expressed his doubt about accepting the work as genuine and that it was of such ancient date.[26] And Keith wrote an article in the *Journal of Royal Asiatic Society* in 1916 on the authenticity of the *Kauṭilīya* and claimed the date of its composition as third century AD. This date was probably later accepted by Stein,[27] J. Jolly[28] and Winternitz.[29]

The third century AD date of the *Arthaśāstra* (or such other later dates—later than the fourth century BC) has been so thoroughly discussed by various scholars that it is unnecessary to go into all the details here. Not only that, in the arguments that follow there may not be much that has not been said before. However, while discussing the date of the *Arthaśāstra* it is hardly possible to leave this aspect of the subject totally out of consideration. Therefore, this part of the question may be stated here briefly.

Four types of arguments have been used by the scholars who have tried to prove that the date of composition of the *Arthaśāstra* is third century AD. The first type maintains that the person known as Kauṭilya is just a legendary name who never really existed. The second type holds that, even if there was such a person, the *Arthaśāstra* was not written by him. The third type tries to prove that the person who wrote the *Arthaśāstra* did not do so during the reign of Candragupta Maurya, i.e. in the fourth century BC. The fourth type tries to show that the *Arthaśāstra* was written in the third century AD. Let us discuss each of these arguments separately.

(a) Existence of Kauṭilya denied

The contention that there was no such person as Kauṭilya is based wholly on a class of arguments called *argumentum ex silentio,* which Kane calls non-mention arguments. According to it, if a writer is silent about some fact or idea or event, that is taken to indicate that he must have been unaware of them, or that there could not have been any knowledge of that fact or idea or event during the period the writer was writing. Such arguments are usually emphasized and adopted by one when they suit one's case, though they ordinarily do not really prove anything, because if a fact or an idea is not mentioned somewhere that does not necessarily mean that that idea or fact did not exist or was not known at that time.

(*i*) In this case the most important point to which our attention is drawn is that the Greek reports on Sandrakottos nowhere refer to Kauṭilya,[30] even though Megasthenes's report is available only in fragments. Whereas the other Greek reports are of a much later period, and so, if Kauṭilya is not mentioned there that does not prove that he did not exist. However, this point shall be taken up again at the end of this section.

(*ii*) Similar argument is advanced by Sir R.G. Bhandarkar[31] and also taken up by some others,[32] namely that though Patañjali in his *Mahābhāṣya* refers to the Maurya and the *Sabhā* of Candragupta, Kauṭilya is not mentioned. *Mahābhāṣya* is not a historical work. It is a treatise on grammar and only such facts are mentioned there by Patañjali as have some connection with grammatical rules. Therefore, if Kauṭilya is not mentioned there that is immaterial.

(*iii*) It is also argued that the *Arthaśāstra* in its genuine portion (Winternitz)[33] does not say anything about the Nandas, the Mauryas, or of king Candragupta or Pāṭaliputra. 'We have to admit that in Ancient India references to contemporary events in works of any kind are, as a rule, hard to find. And in the case of scientific works, which often claimed to be based on the teaching of some mythical sage, if not to the Creator himself, a reference to any contemporary event or person would appear to be almost inconceivable.'[34] Again, what is genuine and what is fake in a work is difficult to determine and every part of a work which is ordinarily found in manuscripts should be accepted as genuine.

(*iv*) Winternitz has one more argument:[35] that all that is said about Kauṭilya is based on hearsay and is based on *Mudrārākṣasa* (a drama), *Kathāsaritsāgara* (a story book in which the introductory story refers to Kauṭilya), and Hemacandra's *Pariśiṣṭa-parvan* (where there are marvellous stories about Kauṭilya). However, even in works of fiction, whether they are novels or plays or story books, history is usually fused with fiction; therefore, the historical elements in such works are not to be totally disregarded. In this connection, we may think of the historical plays of Shakespeare; the historicity of the characters of those dramas has been accepted.

(*v*) Another argument put forward by Jolly[36] is that if the minister Rākṣasa of *Mudrārākṣasa* is probably a myth, why not then is also Kauṭilya a myth? Of course, Jolly has the word 'probably' to modify the word 'myth', but this type of saving grace is usually adopted by Western scholars, Max Müller included, when they state their conclusion hesitatingly. What they actually want is to thrust their contentions down the throat of the reader as facts (cf. Max Müller's statement regarding his Vedic dating that he is simply advancing a hypothesis, or that what he is saying is just as an experiment[37]). Jolly has, however, not stated anywhere what arguments he has for considering Rākṣasa to be a myth and, though

Rākṣasa has rarely been mentioned anywhere else, because the various events about Cāṇakya and Candragupta till the latter's coronation are mainly related in this drama, the existence of Rākṣasa has not been denied anywhere either. Any way, to consider Kauṭilya as a mere myth, simply on the analogy of Rākṣasa, is totally unjustified as Kauṭilya (or Cāṇakya's) existence and his relations with Candragupta have been attested to at a number of places.

(b) *Arthaśāstra*: Not written by Kauṭilya

The scholars mentioned above also hold that, even if Kauṭilya was there as a guide and mentor of Candragupta Maurya, (they wrongly call him Candragupta's minister following Shamsastri), he was not the writer of the *Arthaśāstra*.

(*i*) One reason for this, which sounds quite strange, is given by Winternitz.[38] He says that though the *purāṇas* speak of Kauṭilya (they do not here even mention him by his synonym Cāṇakya or Viṣṇugupta) as having placed Candragupta of the Maurya dynasty on the throne, they know nothing about him as a teacher or as an author; that is unless they had positively spoken of Kauṭilya that he was the writer of the *Arthaśāstra,* he could not have been its author. Actually the *purāṇas* do not give a detailed account of the reign of Candragupta or of the life of Kauṭilya. Ordinarily one verse (*śloka*) or two there refer to Kauṭilya and Candragupta, but what Winternitz avers is that even in this limited reference the *purāṇas* should have clearly stated that this Kauṭilya was also an author and that it was he who wrote the work named *Arthaśāstra* and since that was not done Kauṭilya cannot be said to have been a writer, much less the author of the *Arthaśāstra*. This is not enough. However, the mention by the *purāṇas* of the fact that it was Kauṭilya who destroyed the Nandas and placed Candragupta on the throne is indicative of the fact that they are referring to the writer of the *Arthaśāstra*. Similarly, Winternitz adds (though, of course, a little later)[39] that Somadeva's *Kathāsaritsāgara* (a storybook), the *Mudrārākṣasa* and Hemachandra's *Pariśiṣṭaparvan,* even though they contain stories about Kauṭilya, they were but hearsay and there is no mention in them of Kauṭilya as being a teacher or an author. Winternitz would have been satisfied, it seems, about the veracity of Kauṭilya's being a teacher and an author only if all these works mentioned specifically that Kauṭilya was a teacher and a writer who 'in his leisure hours or perhaps in his old age'[40] wrote a theoretical work, called the *Arthaśāstra*. However, these stories about Kauṭilya were included in these works only for a limited purpose, viz. to describe the public life of Kauṭilya and to emphasize the fact (as in the *purāṇas*) that Kauṭilya destroyed the Nandas and placed Candragupta on the throne, and, in the case of *Mudrārākṣasa,* that Kauṭilya destroyed all the supporters of Nanda or the opponents of Candragupta, and gained the support of the very sincere Rākṣasa for Candragupta as his chief minister. Keith also says, 'We have not the slightest reference there (in *Mudrārākṣasa*) or elsewhere to his literary activity.'[41] However, when one looks into the subject-matter of these works (mentioned above) one sees no occasion there to make references to Kauṭilya's literary activity, because, as Keith himself says, the *Arthaśāstra* was written by 'this alleged statesman meditating in his days of retirement on the maxims of policy'[42], and who, as Winternitz also, referring to Jacobi, says (about Kauṭilya) that he wrote 'a theoretical work (the *Arthaśāstra*) in his old age or perhaps in his leisure hours exactly as Friedrich the Great had done'.

(*ii*) Though the *purāṇas* and the *Kathāsaritsāgara* of Somadeva etc. do not speak of Kauṭilya as having written the *Arthaśāstra*, there are some statements in the *Kauṭilīya* itself which positively assert that Kauṭilya was the writer of the work. These statements have already been referred to above but a brief recapitulation of them here may be helpful. They are: (i) I.1.19, which mentions the *śāstra* composed by Kauṭilya; (ii) II.10.63, which lays down the rules made by Kauṭilya about commandments issued for the sake of the king (*Kauṭilyena narendrārthe śāsanasya vidhiḥ kṛtaṃ*); (iii) the verse after the last colophon at the end which says that the aphorisms (*sūtras*) and the gloss over it (*bhāṣya*) have been composed by Viṣṇugupta himself; and, last XV.1.73, where, though no name has been given, there is a reference to this *sūtra* as having been composed by him who revived the science and the weapon (army) and freed the earth from the domination of the Nanda kings. This clearly refers to Cāṇakya. Thus these references, apart from emphasizing the fact that the *Arthaśāstra* was written by Kauṭilya, mention three aliases of him—the *gotra* name Kauṭilya, the personal name Viṣṇugupta and the parental name Cāṇakya (son of Caṇaka), the first two directly, and the last indirectly. These statements are the main points that refute the contention of the above-mentioned scholars, that, not Kauṭilya, but some other person was the author of the *Arthaśāstra*. Therefore, they have to find a way of convincingly showing that what is indicated in these statements is not true.

Winternitz expresses the view (mentioned earlier) that these are later additions, i.e. they do not belong to the genuine portion of the *Kauṭilīya Arthaśāstra*.[43] Not only that, he holds that the chapters in which these stanzas occur do not belong to the original text and were probably added in the final redaction.[44] But he does not confine himself to this alone. He adds that 'in the work itself the author has been mentioned as Cāṇakya Viṣṇugupta though he is otherwise always referred to as Kauṭilya' and it is improbable that a person will call himself by this name which means 'falsehood' and 'crookedness'. So he considers these statements to be spurious. Now, firstly, it is difficult to say what is genuine and what is not genuine in a treatise. What is concluded in this regard depends on the personal whim of a scholar, and, secondly, Kauṭilya is a *gotra* name as stated by the commentary *Upādhyāyanirpekṣā* of the *Kāmandakīya*. Now, this commentary existed much before Jolly or Winternitz wrote. Therefore, Kauṭilya is not 'cunning personified', as Jolly says[45], but is a *gotra* name, and this fact is repeatedly stressed by Kane.[46]

Jolly believes that only one of these verses is a later addition—the verse XV.1.73 (78, according to his edited text) because it 'was added by the author in accordance with tradition which credited Kauṭilya with the overthrow of the Nandas and with the foundation of the science of polity.'[47] About one other verse, the one after the last colophon and ascribed to Viṣṇugupta, Jolly is uncertain whether it is to be ascribed to the author or to someone else.[48] He is silent about two other verses. Thus, though not denying the originality of most of these verses, Jolly does not however think that Kauṭilya or Cāṇakya is the author of the *Arthaśāstra*. His reason for this is that Pāṭaliputra, the capital, is nowhere mentioned in the work and gems from South India and Sri Lanka occupy a prominent place[49] in it, and the trade route to the South is considered to be preferable,[50] which probably, according to Jolly, shows that the writer came from the South whereas Kauṭilya was from the North. As regards not mentioning Pāṭaliputra, Kangle's explanation, already referred to, points out that these works do not refer to the conditions of the time.[51] The second question regarding the writer's belonging to the South will be discussed presently (p. 25).

Keith was the first among these three scholars to take up this point. He does not seem to have any cogent reason for not accepting the verses as authentic, i.e. original. However, he denies Kauṭilya's authorship of the *Arthaśāstra* because, according to him, in the last Book under the explanation of *apadeśa*, a *tantrayukti* (an expedient in the writing of science), one of Kauṭilya's sentences is cited which shows that Kauṭilya is regarded as an authority, and not as an author[52]; so Kauṭilya is not the author. Keith then proceeds, in the next paragraph, to express doubts as to Kauṭilya's being a historic character mainly because Megasthenes does not mention him (and such other instances of non-mention). He also expresses doubts about Kauṭilya's literary activity because there is no reference to it in the *Mudrārākṣasa* and elsewhere. It has already been explained above that not mentioning Kauṭilya by Megasthenes and by other Greek writers is not a convincing proof that he did not exist during the reign of Candragupta, for *Mudrārākṣasa* and other works were written simply to show how Kauṭilya's helping Candragupta enabled him to gain and make secure his throne and so no reference to Kauṭilya's literary activity was needed there.[53] The point about *Apadeśa* will be taken up below(pp. 23–24). There is nothing in what Keith says to make one accept that the author of *Arthaśāstra* was someone other than Kauṭilya.

(*iii*) Another factor that impedes these writers from proving their point is the use of *'iti Kauṭilyaḥ'* and *'neti Kauṭilyaḥ'* at several places in the text of the *Arthaśāstra*. On the basis of the opinions of Kauṭilya expressed in the third person, the view is put forward by Hillebrandt that it is not the work of Kauṭilya but of a school,[54] and this is also the opinion of Keith[55] and Winternitz.[56] But Kane says: 'In order to avoid looking too egotistical ancient writers generally put their own views in the third person', and he quotes Medhātithi: '*Prāyeṇa granthakārāḥ svamataṃ parāpdeśena bruvate*' and also Viśvarūpa[57], a commentator of the *Yājñavalkyasmṛti*. Not only this, he holds that had it been the work of a school it would have been '*iti Kauṭilyāḥ*' instead of '*iti Kauṭilyaḥ*'.

(*iv*) Another ground for saying that the *Arthaśāstra* is not the work of Kauṭilya is one (9th) *tantrayukti* (out of 32), *apadeśa*, about which Keith's opinion has been stated above. This *tantrayukti*, as found in the *Arthaśāstra*[58], is 'So and so said such and such' is reference (Kangle's translation of the word *apadeśa*, but 'statement' according to Apte's Dictionary). (He) should appoint a council of ministers (consisting) of twelve ministers, according to Mānavas. Sixteen, according to Bārhaspatyas. Twenty, according to Auśanasas. As is found adequate, according to Kauṭilya.'[59] Jolly wrongly translated *Apadeśa* as 'statement of the views of others' on the basis of IV.8.2 where it is stated that the accused should be questioned about his country, caste, family, etc., and that his statement should be compared with the statement (*apadeśa*) (of others). Here under the word *apadeśa*, the words 'of others' are kept understood. This is clear from Kangle's translation, but also from the meaning of the word in Apte's Sanskrit-English Dictionary. In Sanskrit passages some words remain understood as (he) and (consisting) in the passage on *apadeśa* (I.15. 47-50) whose translation has been quoted above. So *apadeśa* only means statement and not 'statement of others' as translated by Jolly. Jolly, according to his own translation, wrongly concludes that Kauṭilya's opinions in the *Arthaśāstra*, not only in the passage given here (i.e. I.15. 47–50) as an example of *apadeśa*, but also at 80 other odd places, where the words '*iti Kauṭilyaḥ*' or '*neti Kauṭilyaḥ*' are used are *apadeśa* and, therefore, they would not represent author's own views.

The conclusion of Jolly seems to be manifestly misleading.[60] Keith draws another conclusion that here 'Kauṭilya is cited as an authority, not as the author'.[61] But Kauṭilya is here both an authority, as he expresses an authoritative view and also an author, and that there is no contradiction in one's being both an author and an authority. Therefore, *apadeśa* in no way proves that Kauṭilya was not the author of the *Arthaśāstra*.

(*v*) Another ground for denying the authorship of the *Arthaśāstra* to Kauṭilya is that it is the work of a *paṇḍita*. 'In the *Arthaśāstra,* we find the same predilection for definition, pedantic division, classification and schematization as in other scientific works written by *paṇḍitas*.'[62] This means that it is not composed by one who played an active role in statecraft. On the other hand, those who think otherwise have emphatically argued that learned treatises have also been written by people who have played an active part in the politics of their countries, and instances have been given of Sāyaṇa and Mādhava at Vijayanagar and of Hemādri who worked with Yādava kings. And not only in India, but elsewhere also, President Wilson and George Stanley McGovern, a politician (a candidate in the 1972 presidential election) in the U.S.A., and Lord Morley in England are twentieth century examples among those who have not only written learned books, but also played a successful role in politics.

(*vi*) Another reason advanced against the generally accepted tradition that Kauṭilya composed the *Arthaśāstra* is that the rules of the *Arthaśāstra* relate to a moderate-sized state, whereas Candragupta Maurya ruled over an empire. This argument is correct in the sense that ancient Indian states were usually small in size, and even the more powerful ones were not very large, though they exercised suzerainty over others of comparable size. This is what is meant by a *vijigīṣu* or *sārvabhauma* or *cakravartin* and the *maṇḍala* theory. The theoretical conception of an empire in ancient India was a state that exercised suzerainty over similar other states; therefore, Kauṭilya's conception of the state does not mean that he had nothing to do with the empire of Candragupta Maurya.

(*vii*) Another argument of these Western scholars is that the author of the *Arthaśāstra* was from the South and as Kauṭilya belonged to the North he could not have been its author. This is the view mainly of Jolly. 'The geographical horizon of the author, on the whole points to a southern rather than to a northern home.'[63] The reasons given for it are that gems from South India occupy a prominent place in the work[64], that the route to the South is considered preferable to that to the North[65], that the only known manuscripts of the *Arthaśāstra* exist in the South, and that frequent interchange of two letters, *va* and *pa* in the same manuscripts is a southern peculiarity.[66] But Keith is not so particular about these points. 'The author may have lived in the South' since 'South Indian and Ceylonese gems bulk largely in the chapter on gems, but this is a conjecture, for the fact that manuscripts exist only in the South is not of much importance.' However, it does not seem that Kauṭilya shows any partiality towards any area. He praises prized goods from any part of the world. Horses are preferred from Kāmboja (north of Gāndhāra, i.e. Afghanistan), Sindhu, Āraṭṭa (Punjab) and Vanāyu (Arabia according to some and Persia according to others)[67], but among gems, diamonds from Vidharbha, Kaliṅga, Kośala and Kāśi are preferred.[68] Some goods from Himālaya, are preferred, others from Burma or Sumatra.[69] While *dukūla* (cloth of a special type) from Vaṅga is considered good[70], coral from Vivarṇa, i.e. Yavanadvīpa,[71] and silk from the Māgadhas and Kāśmīra are noted for their good quality.[72]

As regards the trade-route, not only is the route to the south preferred to that to the north but, similarly, the route to the west is preferred to that to the east.[73] All these should make it evident that no final decision on these grounds can be taken about the writer's home.

(*viii*) Another ground for denying the authorship of *Arthaśāstra* to Kauṭilya is that several works are referred to as having been authored by Cāṇakya or Vṛddha Cāṇakya because, according to Winternitz, 'Cāṇakya or Kauṭilya is the model of the most famous type of cunning and unscrupulous minister, who is, however, faithful to his master, whom we meet so often in the dramatic and narrative literature beginning from Bhāsa.'[74] The same opinion is held by Jolly.[75] It is, of course, true that several works of epigrams are held to have been written by Cāṇakya or Vṛddha Cāṇakya, but, as accepted by Winternitz in the next sentence after his quotation above, this was a later process. So it cannot be applied to the *Arthaśāstra*. Not only this. While Kauṭilya and his *Arthaśāstra* have been referred to in several places, there is no mention of the other works in any other place. So the *Arthaśāstra* of Kauṭilya is far more authoritative than the other works and to say that just as these works have been shown to be by Cāṇakya, similarly the *Arthaśāstra*, though not authored by Kauṭilya, is wrongly called the *Kauṭilīya*. This is a correlation which cannot be justified on the grounds stated here.

(*ix*) Such *ślokas* in the *Arthaśāstra* as are concerned with ascribing the authorship of the work have not been accepted as such by Keith, Jolly and Winternitz. Winternitz doubts the genuineness of these stanzas, while Keith and Jolly have raised some arguments in support of their view that *Arthaśāstra* was not composed by Kauṭilya. As for the words *'iti Kauṭilyaḥ'* and *'neti Kauṭilyaḥ'*, according to Hillebrandt, Keith and Winternitz, they do not show that the *Arthaśāstra* is a work by Kauṭilya, but that it was composed by a school; Keith and Jolly think that the expression *tantrayukti Apadeśa* shows that the *Arthaśāstra* is not Kautilya's work. However, none of these scholars take similar views about another statement in the *Arthaśāstra*, viz., what the colophons say at the end of every book, that it is the *Kauṭilīya Arthaśāstra*. This is somewhat grudgingly allowed by Jolly.[76] Jolly holds, as we have seen, that the *Arthaśāstra* was authored, not by Kauṭilya but by someone else from the South; so he tries to explain the contrary record mentioned in the colophons by making the strange suggestion that his 'real' author may have ascribed the authorship of the whole or part of the treatise to Kauṭilya. However, nowhere does Jolly explain why the real author of such an important work would wish to ascribe the authorship to some other person. Keith and Winternitz have not put up even this excuse regarding the mention of the words *'Kauṭilīya Arthaśāstra'* in the colophons, so, it would seem like the other passages mentioned above, they could not explain away these expressions to show that the *Arthaśāstra* is not the work of Kauṭilya. We may therefore maintain without any danger of contradiction either from Keith and Winternitz, and even from Jolly, that these statements in the colophons, are sufficient to demonstrate that Kauṭilya is the author of the *Arthaśāstra*.

(*x*) The statements in the *Daśakumāracarita*[77], in the *Tantrākhyāyikā* and the *Pañcatantra*[78], in *Kādambarī*[79], in the *Nandisūtra* and *Anuyogadvāra* in the Jaina canon[80] and in the *Kāmandakīya*[81] *Nītisāra* have been accepted by these scholars and show that the *Arthaśāstra* is the work of Kauṭilya, although they have made attempts to prove that it is a late work belonging to the third century AD. What is attempted to be stressed here is that in spite of some preliminary objections to some *ślokas* of the *Arthaśāstra*, mainly by Winternitz[82], and to *'iti Kauṭilyaḥ'* and *'neti Kauṭilyaḥ'* as expressing Kauṭilya's authorship of the *Arthaśāstra*, and in spite of their exploiting the *tantrayukti apadeśa* to prove this, they could not deny the authorship of the treatise to Kauṭilya because of the statement in the colophons and because of references to Kauṭilya's or Viṣṇugupta's or Cāṇakya's work in several other treatises. This was done by Trautmann in his *Kauṭilya and the Arthaśāstra*, as directed by Basham. The second part of this article will be devoted to examining the points sought to be established in that book based mainly on statistical analysis.

(c) *Arthaśāstra*: Not a work of fourth century BC

Thirdly, there are other facts which, according to the above mentioned scholars' contention show that the *Arthaśāstra* was not composed in the fourth century BC and that if its author was Kauṭilya, he did not live then. (i) The most important argument put forward in support of this thesis, as already discussed, is that Megasthenes does not mention Kauṭilya, which he certainly would have done had Kauṭilya lived during Candragupta's reign. As against this, it is contended that only fragments of Megasthenes's work have been found. It cannot therefore be firmly said that Megasthenes did not know Kauṭilya. Moreover, this is just an *argumentum ex silentio* and as such it has little validity to prove the case.

Apart from this, doubts have been expressed by Western scholars about the reliability of Megasthenes's testimony. Jolly says, 'The idealistic tendency in Megasthenes greatly impairs the trustworthiness of his statements', and he gives as examples a number of unrealistic and idealistic statements made by Megasthenes: that Indians keep no slaves; that all men among them are considered equal; that agriculturists are not persecuted even in times of war, nor are their cultivated fields devastated by belligerents; that Indians never drink wines except at the time of sacrifices; that Indians do not involve in litigation over pledges and deposits, and they require neither seals nor witnesses; that houses and properties of Indians are generally left unguarded and thefts are rare.[83] Stein also doubts some of Megasthenes's statements such as the existence of a royal highway of 10000 stadia, i.e. about 1000 miles (from Takṣilā to Pāṭaliputra, probably the one presently known as the Grand Trunk Road), or the width of a moat being 177 metres, or of Megasthenes's not referring to king's harem.[84]

Jolly accepts some other statements made by Megasthenes, mainly those which are contrary to what is found in the *Arthaśāstra,* viz., that Indians did not know the art of writing, that they knew only five kinds of metals, that in Candragupta's reign there were few taxes. If some of Megathenese's statements are considered doubtful, so can also be others (see points ii, iv and v below). There should be an objective criteria for evaluating these statements and not simply the testimony of Jolly and Stein.[85] And the fact that Megasthenes does not mention Kauṭilya cannot be taken as a final proof that he (Kauṭilya) did not exist during Candragupta Maurya's reign.

(*ii*) Jolly thinks that, according to Megasthenes, Indians did not then know the art of writing, while the '*Arthaśāstra* mentions books, letters and passports, registration and correspondence, clerks and accountants and devotes an entire chapter to the production of royal writs (II.10)'.[86] Kane says that no Western writer would now say that writing was unknown to the Indians in 320 BC.[87] More important than this is what Bühler says about the existence of writing and written documents in India in connection with the *Vasiṣṭha Dharmasūtra* whose date has been assigned by Kane to the fourth century BC or earlier[88], probably in accordance with what Bühler has written about that *Smṛti* in the Introduction to its translation. Quoting some portions from that passage is necessary in order to understand what Bühler says about a later date for the *Dharmasūtra* because of the mention of written documents in it. Bühler contends:[89] 'Nor will it be advisable to adduce the fact that Vasiṣṭha XVI.10, 15 mentions written documents as a means of legal proof in order to establish a 'comparatively late' date of the *Sūtras*.' Writing in 1882 he says, 'The proofs for the antiquity of the Indian alphabets are now much stronger than they were even a short time ago'. He continues that the other *Dharmasūtras*, e.g. Āpastamba, are silent about written documents because 'those points only fall primarily within the scope of the *Dharmasūtras* which have some immediate close connection with the *Dharma*. . . . Judicial technicalities like the determination of the legal value of written documents had less importance and were left either to the *deśācāra*, the custom of the country or to the *nīti* and *arthaśāstras*,' and not because writing was unknown in India at their time.

(*iii*) Kauṭilya's mention of the use of Sanskrit in royal edicts is considered to be another ground for saying that the *Arthaśāstra* was not produced in the fourth century BC because Sanskrit edicts came into use later than the Prakrit edicts. However, Sanskrit is an older language than Pali and, therefore, it cannot be accepted that the use of Sanskrit edicts was later than that of Pali edicts. Says Kangle[90], 'Sanskrit certainly existed before Prakrit came into being, and its use must have long preceded that of Prakrit. This must have been the case particularly when learning of any sort was in question'. For Sanskrit, Jacobi puts the matter in the form of an answer to the following question:

'How far the use of classical Sanskrit prevailed in the early centuries before the Christian era?' He explains it by saying that the earliest inscriptions of Aśoka and of others in the following centuries were written only in Prakrit. Therefore, 'it has been concluded that Sanskrit originated much later in the Brahmanical schools and remained for a long time as a learned language, it attained a more extensive character till from the fourth and fifth centuries AD it became the literary language of the whole of India'. Jacobi does not subscribe to this argument because (a) the language of the ancient epics was Sanskrit. And (b), with regard to the *Arthaśāstra* he says that 'thousands of things—ideas, conditions, etc. of common political and economic life find expression in that work in Sanskrit, not in Prakrit. The conclusion holds good not only for the time of Kauṭilya, but also for the preceding period during which came into existence those works of his predecessors which he has quoted and utilized.' Similarly *Kāmasūtra* did not remain confined to the priestly class, and not only Vātsyāyana but his predecessors also wrote in Sanskrit ...'otherwise Vātsyāyana would certainly have preferred the claim of being the first to teach his science in Sanskrit'. This was also the case with the *Dharmaśāstras*. 'Herein occurs the consideration of the most diverse facts of practical life, the knowledge and understanding of which would be found least of all in the priestly schools.' Thus *dharma, artha* and *kāma* which referred to all men and not to the learned only found expression in Sanskrit. Not only this, (c) he also holds that Sanskrit was the official language which the prince used in his letters and decrees. They were prepared, according to the chapter *śāsanādhikāra* by a *lekhaka* who was to have the qualifications of an *amātya*.[91] His qualifications included *śāstracakṣuṣmattā*[92], i.e. he should thoroughly understand the language of science.

'The knowledge of different languages was not ordained, as would necessarily have been the case had diplomatic correspondence been carried on in Prakrit.' According to Jacobi, diplomatic correspondence included not only inter-state correspondence, but also all writs/orders and communications *śāsanas*,[93] except to inferior persons.[94]

(*iv*) One more argument advanced by Keith, Jolly and Winternitz to show that the *Arthaśāstra* was composed after the fourth century BC, is that at the time of the *Arthaśāstra* 'Metallurgy and mining industries were highly developed, the working of metals was a state monopoly and lay in the hands of officials.... Against this, Megasthenes refers to five kinds of metals produced in India and Strabo describes the Indians as inexperienced in the arts of mining and melting.'[95] It is no doubt true that in India mining was a state monopoly, but sometimes this operation was leased out for exploitation[96]. Besides Megasthenes also speaks of 'other metals' other than these five and Diodoros confirms this.[97] According to Ktesias and Curtius, India produced steel of high quality[98] and according to Rostovtzeff[99] this type of steel of Indian origin was borrowed from there by Asia Minor.

(*v*) In support of a late date of composition of the *Arthaśāstra,* Stein mentioned another discrepancy in the accounts given by Megasthenes and Kauṭilya, and this point is also taken up by Jolly, Keith[100] and Winternitz[101]. This is that while Megasthenes mentions only a few taxes, Kauṭilya mentions a large number of them. This argument is however not tenable. In the *Arthaśāstra* Kauṭilya mentions the sources of income at various places.[102] In 'Taxation in the *Kauṭilīya Arthaśāstra*' the author[103] has analyzed in detail the sources of income and the conclusion arrived at is that the taxes are only those mentioned in I.13.6, and these include *bhāga* (share), *śulka* (duties), *kara* (tax) and labour in place of taxes, though it can be considered a part of *bhāga* itself. Share includes one-sixth part of the agricultural produce[104] and one-sixth part of fish and birds and beasts[105] acquired for selling. Duty includes duty (*śulka*) on export and import of goods[106] and excise duty.[107] Import duty is different for different goods[108] and excise duty is customary. *Hiraṇyakara* is ten per cent.[109] These are taxes. Apart from this there are monopoly charges, service charges and license fees; they are not taxes. Monopoly charges are income from mines and forests[110] and from coining and salt.[111] This is state income and this also includes income from state lands, state factories and animals owned by the state.[112] Service charges (e.g., railway fares and irrigation charges as now) include charges for providing protection[113] and irrigation facilities.[114] License fees (e.g., licenses for buses and to prostitutes as at present) are for carrying on animal slaughter[115] or for preparing spirituous liquor[116] or from public women.[117] Thus, though in the *Arthaśāstra* a large number of sources of income for the state are mentioned, the number of taxes is limited—and they are only those which are found in the *Manusmṛti*.[118] Megasthenes also mentions mostly these taxes, 'a land tax, a tax on river gold, and taxes on herdsmen and artisans and on articles sold'.[119]

(*vi*) The idea that the word *suruṅga* is derived from the Greek *syrinx* is borrowed by most writers from Stein.[120] Keith says that it is no doubt so. He also gives the date of that borrowing as not until after the Christian era.[121] It can be clearly seen that there is not much similarity soundwise between *suruṅga* and *syrinx*. Both Keith and Jolly[122] say that *suruṅga* means a mine, though the primary meaning of the word is a 'subterranean passage' and even if it means 'a mine dug under a house' (both the meanings from Apte's Dictionary), it carries the sense of a tunnel. On the other hand, *syṛinx,* according to Tarn,[123] means a mine or a covered gallery for attacking a town. Therefore, neither because of the meaning nor for the similarity of sound, can *syrinx* be equated with *suruṅga.* Moreover, most scholars are not prepared to accept a Greek origin for *suruṅga.* They suggest that it is originally from the Babylonian or Santal word *surun* which means a hole.[124]

(*vii*) Trautmann thinks that 'Its (*Arthaśāstra's*) geographical horizons are broader than what seems likely for the Mauryan period, and a number of place-names in the second book are late'[125], and he refers to Cīna, Tāmraparṇi, Ālakanda, Hārahūraka and Prājjunaka. Of these Ālakanda, Hārahūraka and Prājjunaka lay beyond the North-Western frontier of India. However, according to various scholars, Indians not only knew, but also had regular contact with the people of the West. A.H. Sayce says that as far back as the third millennium BC, there was cultural and possibly racial continuity between Babylon and Punjab.[126] Peacocks, rice and Indian sandalwood were known in Palestine under their Tamil names in the Book of Genesis and the Books of Kings.[127] The Bogozkei inscription of about 1400 BC, recording treaties between the king of Hittites and the king of Mitanni, shows that the dynasties of the latter period had the Vedic gods Indra, Varuṇa, Mitra and Nāstya in their pantheon.[128] Sayce[129] 'draws attention to the fact that Hittite numerals like sika, tere, panz, satta, nawa are Sanskrit and also *aika-wartanna* (one turn) and concludes that in Mesopotamia and East Asia Minor lived a people that spoke Sanskrit'. The Baveru Jataka[130] refers to trade by sea between Babylonia and India. 'Strabo[131] states that an embassy from King Pandion (Pāṇḍya) was received in the West and that an Indian embassy brought to King Augustus a letter from its king in Greek written on parchment.' Asoka's edict No. 13[132] refers to five kings of the Near East to whom Buddhist missionaries had been sent, viz., to Antiyoga (Antiochus of Syria), Jurmaya (Ptolemy II of Egypt), Antikina (Antigonus of Macedonia), Maga (Magus of Cyrene), and Aliksundara of Epirus.'[133] As regards China, Jacobi states: 'It may be mentioned that among extra-Indian countries I have found mention of China only. That in II.11 (114) are mentioned the silk fabrics (*Kauśeyaṃ cīnapattāśca cīnabhūmijā*) which are produced in the country of China. This makes it certain that China bore the name Cīna in 300 BC, which finally disposes of the derivation of the word China from the dynasty of Thsin (247 BC)'.[134] It may be noted that China is still famous for its silk, and that silk is imported into India.

(*viii*) Another argument for a late date of composition of the *Arthaśāstra,* however unimportant and without much substantiation, is that the different subjects dealt with in the second *Adhikaraṇa* of the *Arthaśāstra* and at other places also, for example, in the tenth (war) and the fourteenth books (magic practices, etc.), could not have been mastered by a single person. Jolly and his companion writers hold that the supposition that this knowledge was derived from 'fellow experts' or officer collaborators is not correct, and that on the basis of the first sentence of the book[135] it was derived from earlier texts on these subjects and so the work may have been composed at quite a later date. Jolly[136] is, in the beginning, the least assertive among the three scholars. He says, 'Some chapters of the second *adhikaraṇa* may be based on the special treatises', and that 'we do not know how much of Kauṭilya's work may be due to his predecessors in the field of *Arthaśāstra*'. Winternitz argues in a slightly more detailed manner: 'It may be assumed that when Kauṭilya wrote these chapters he had officers as his collaborators. But it is more probable that there had existed special works on individual topics that were adopted with little alteration by the author of the *Arthaśāstra* in his work. . . . From this it follows that the origin of the *Kauṭilīya Arthaśāstra* must presuppose a prolonged literary activity not only in the field of politics but also in different branches of the technical sciences and economics'.[137] Keith, though brief, is the most assertive.[138] Jolly concludes that this 'work is the outcome of a long period of literary activity in the field of polity, rather than the production of a creative genius, another reason for not fixing its age-limit too high'.[139] Now, it may be argued that Marx's socialist ideas are also the culmination of a long period of socialistic or communistic thinking from Plato down to modern socialist thought which begins with the French Revolution. Marx is modest enough to admit that there is not much in his thinking that is new. 'What I did that was new was to prove (1) that the existence of classes is only bound up with historical phases in the development of production; (2) that the class struggle necessarily leads to the dictatorship of the proletariat; (3) that this dictatorship itself only constitutes the transition to the abolition of all classes and to a classless society.' Thus, according to Marx, the idea of the exploitation of the weaker sections of the society by the upper classes, the idea of the class struggle and of a socialist order of society was not originally his. Yet even his severest critics have not said that Marx was no creative genius. The combination of all previous ideas in a new mould is itself the work of a creative genius, and this is what Kauṭilya did.

So it is wrong to suppose that this literary activity could not have preceded the fourth century BC. Some political ideas found in the *Kauṭilīya* are also found in Vedic literature and to a greater extent in the *Dharmasūtras*[140], in the *Rāmāyaṇa* and the *Mahābhārata,* about which Jolly erroneously assumes that its *rājadharma* 'is in an embryonic condition as compared to the detailed provisions and advanced conditions of life in the *Arthaśāstra'*,[141] and in the *Manusmṛti.*[142] Thus even if no other works earlier than the fourth century BC can be found, the works just mentioned above are by themselves sufficient literary activity that preceded the *Arthaśāstra,* even if the *Arthaśāstra* belongs to the fourth century BC.

As regards Winternitz's contention that much literary activity even in the technical sciences preceded the *Kauṭilīya,* and that that may have been even before the fourth century BC, what Kauṭilya actually says is that he drew his material from other works on the science of politics (only) which were composed for the acquisition and protection of the earth.[143] This is also what Kāmandaka says, that Kauṭilya extracted the nectar of *nītiśāstra* from the *Arthaśāstra* works.[144] Therefore, the possibility is that the material about other technical sciences was collected by Kauṭilya not so much from other treatises on those subjects as through his association with those who were engaged in that kind of work.

(*ix*) Jolly has given another reason for assigning the late date of composing the *Arthaśāstra,* but that will be dealt with in detail because that reason is used not only for proving that the *Arthaśāstra* was not composed in the fourth century BC, but that is also connected with his conclusion that the work was composed in the third century AD. Trautmann also refers to this argument of Jolly. Jolly holds that 'Generally speaking the *Dharmaśāstra* or science of duty and religion has far better claims to a high antiquity than the *Arthaśāstra* or science of gain which in its turn is older than the *Kāmaśāstra* or the science of love, the three sciences based on *trivarga* have followed each other in point of time as well as in rank and value. Vedic religion bore an essentially religious character, and secular topics such as those treated in the *Arthaśāstra* must have appeared unimportant or even wicked to the ancient *ṛṣis*'.[145] Jolly continues:[146] 'The superior antiquity of the role of the *Dharmaśāstra* is borne out by a consideration of the role of the general development of the civilization and moral philosophy in India, which was much . . . that of a natural reaction against the high-flown idealism and one-sided religious character of the Vedic lore and literature. . . . Reprehensible practices such as the murder of distinguished officers, the levying of oppressive taxes, the corrupt system of espionage may have existed from an early period, but it was not probably till the rise of a science of *Arthaśāstra* that they were openly recognised and even recommended in Sanskrit literature'.

This whole argument is merely conjectural. There are several parts in it. The first part of the argument is that of the three sciences on *dharma, artha* and *kāma*. The *dharmaśāstra* is the earliest, in point of time, then follows the *Arthaśāstra,* and thereafter the *Kāmaśāstra*. What actually happened one does not know, but Indian tradition has it that works on *dharma, artha* and *kāma* came into existence simultaneously. According to the *Śāntiparva* of the *Mahābhārata,* Brahmā composed a work on *dharma, artha, kāma* and *mokṣa,* from which the work on *nīti* was abridged successively by several writers.[147] The *Kāmasūtra* also says[148] that Prajāpati (Brahmā) composed a treatise from which the portion on *dharma* was abridged by Manu, that on *artha* by Bṛhaspati and that on *Kāma* by Nandi. Whether these stories are correct may be doubted, but this much is certain that, though it is traditionally believed in India that of the three goals of life, *dharma* is the highest, and next comes *artha,* and finally *kāma* in point of importance, yet it is also held that at every period in the life of a society all the three are equally necessary, and, therefore the composition of works on different aspects of *trivarga* at different periods is not considered to be true. In actual fact also the *Śukranīti,* which is an *arthaśāstra,* seems to belong to a period near the *Manusmṛti* because, while every work on *nīti* later than the *Kauṭilīya* has followed it and quoted from it, this is not the case with the *Śukranīti,* which shows that it is earlier than the *Arthaśāstra.*

The second part of the argument is also wrong, for to the ancient *ṛṣis,* secular topics were not unimportant or immoral. In the *Atharvaveda,* there are at least three *sūktas* on *kāma*[149], in the last of which *kāma* itself is highly praised. And in the Vedas, in various verses there are prayers to the effect that God may give the person concerned (king) victory over his enemies. There is mention of spies.[150] In the Ṛgveda, there is a prayer to Indra that the new king may be paid tribute by others[151] and in Vedic literature there are various matters concerned with the state.[152]

The third part of the argument of Jolly that the *Arthaśāstra* was a natural reaction against the idealism and one-sided religious character of the Vedic lore, also seems to be fallacious. A study of the Vedic literature reveals a distinct pragmatism there, because the Vedas are full of prayers for various material things needed for worldly life. This tendency is found, to some extent, even in the Upaniṣads even though they are otherwise highly idealistic. The *Bṛhadāraṇyaka* asserts[153] that the essence of all this world (*bhūta-carācara* according to Śaṅkara) is the semen of man (or male). Prajāpati thought that there should be some receptacle where this semen could stay. So he created a woman and her lower part, so that it could be enjoyed (or used—*upāsana*). He (also) created the organ of generation. Therefore, one should not revile against this (act of the copulation of man and woman). The *Chāndogya* also says[154], 'one is disposed to act when (through it) one obtains (material) happiness, without (the chance) of obtaining happiness one does not act . . . therefore, one should make enquiries about happiness'. Even the *Manusmṛti,* which Jolly considers to be older than the *Arthaśāstra* has such verses as, 'A *snātaka* who is able (to earn) should not suffer from hunger. If (he is) in possession of money (he) should not wear tattered and dirty clothes'[155], whereas, Kauṭilya is not without idealism. He recommends the obtainment of *mokṣa*[156], not only gives *dharma* a very important place[157], not only does he ask the king to remain within moral limits[158], and to live for the good of the subjects[159], but even where he recommends immoral methods, he puts a restriction on them.[160]

The fourth part of Jolly's argument is that as a reaction to the *dharmaśāstra* Kauṭilya asks the king to indulge in such reprehensible practices as the murder of distinguished officers and the levying of oppressive taxes. Even though Jolly has edited the text of the *Arthaśāstra,* he does not appear to have gone through it carefully. The murder of distinguished officers is given in detail in one chapter.[161] Kauṭilya in the beginning (*sūtra* 2) asks the king to win over 'those principal officers who live on the king by holding him in their power or who are in league with the enemy'; or 'to control them by the employment of secret agents'. If this fails only then, Kauṭilya advises, 'Against those treasonable officers, who being favourites or being united cause harm to the state, (and) cannot be suppressed openly, he (i.e. the king), who desires (the establishment) of *dharma,* should employ silent punishment', (*sūtra* 4). At the end of the chapter, after describing in detail the various methods of 'silent punishment', it is said that though the king should employ them without any hesitation, yet the king should also remain forgiving both at the present time as also in the future.[162] These measures are thus recommended as measures of the last resort only when their use becomes absolutely imperative.

As regards highly oppressive taxes, it has already been pointed out above[163] that in the *Kauṭilīya* the number of taxes is limited. Of course, there are service charges as for protection and irrigation, and licence fees for dealers preparing spirituous liquor, or for those engaged in animal slaughter for providing meat, and for prostitutes, as we have them now. None of these sources of income can be called tax or that they are oppressive.[164] The rates of taxes are fixed, and even though in emergencies the state can have increased taxation, even then this increase has been specifically laid down[165], and this 'demand is to be made once only and not twice'.[166] If this does not serve the purpose contributions are to be collected from the subjects.[167] Of course, Kauṭilya points out certain methods of raising money which can be called immoral, but the king is asked to use these methods only against the 'treasonable and unrighteous persons', and not against 'others' and he is warned that, 'he should take from the kingdom fruits as they ripen, as from a garden, he should avoid unripe (ones) that cause an uprising for fear of his own destruction'.[168] It may also be mentioned here that, according to Kauṭilya, the treasury ought to be righteously obtained (*dharmādhigata)*[169], and taxes should be customary.[170] 'He should avoid even a big profit that should be injurious to the subjects'.[171] Oppression of people for raising money is decried.[172] Thus all the four parts of Jolly's argument to prove that the *Kauṭilīya Arthaśāstra* is a reaction against the idealism of the *dharmaśāstras*, and that, therefore, on this ground, it is a late work, fall to the ground.

(d) *Arthaśāstra*: A composition of third century AD

The contention that the *Kauṭilīya Arthaśāstra* was composed in the third century AD is based mainly on the dates assigned by the three above-mentioned scholars to certain treatises as having been composed either before or later than the *Arthaśāstra*. In the former category come the *Mahābhārata* and the different *Smṛtis*, and among the latter, the more important ones are the *Kāmasūtra* (4th century AD), the *Nyāyabhāṣya*, the *Tantrākhyāyikā* (fourth or fifth century AD), the *Nandisūtra* and *Anuyogadvāra sūtras* (Jaina canons of uncertain date), Varāhamihira's *Bṛhatsaṁhitā*, the *Caraka-saṁhitā* and *Kādambarī* (7th century AD), the *Kāmandakīya Nītisāra* (8th century AD and the *Daśakumāra-carita*. The dates put within parenthesis are Jolly's dates.

Apart from these dates used for fixing the *Arthaśāstra's* date as the third century AD, two other arguments have been put forward. One is the use of the word *suruṅga* (by Keith only—partially discussed earlier) and the second is the knowledge of alchemy as recorded in the *Arthaśāstra*, which, according to Jolly, could not have been imported into India before the first centuries of the Christian era. Keith and Winternitz also refer to Jolly for this date. These two points will be taken up at the end of this discussion. Meanwhile, the only point that remains to be tackled here is how far these dates can be considered to be correct, and even if they are correct how far they affect the fourth century BC or the third century AD composition dates of the *Arthaśāstra*. We will discuss the dates in the order they have been mentioned here.

(*i*) The opinion of Jolly[173] and of Winternitz[174] that the main story of the *Mahābhārata* was known when the *Kauṭilīya* was composed is correct. As these writers do not mention any firm date of the *Mahābhārata*, Kane's date of 500 BC[175] as the latest composition date for the core of the

Mahābhārata may be tentatively accepted. So if the *Mahābhārata* was composed in 500 BC, and if the *Kauṭilīya* is later than the *Mahābhārata* there could be no objection to the last quarter of the fourth century BC as the composition date of the *Arthaśāstra*.

(*ii*) Patañjali's date is said to be about 150 BC[176], and the only fact stated about Patañjali in relation to Kauṭilya's date is that in his *Mahābhāṣya* he does not mention either Kauṭilya or the *Arthaśāstra*. But this is an *argumentum ex silentio* which, as we have already pointed out, does not prove anything, and that *Mahābhāṣya* is a book on grammar and not on history has already been mentioned in connection with the arguments on the non-existence of Kauṭilya (point 2, p. 16 above) but what must be stated here is that even if the validity of the argument is accepted it can only prove that Kauṭilya did not live in the fourth century BC, but it cannot in any case prove that the *Arthaśāstra* was written in the third century AD.

(*iii*) After quoting 33 passages that are similar in the *Arthaśāstra* and the different *Smṛtis* (including the *Baudhāyana* and the *Viṣṇu Dharmasūtras*), Jolly concludes[177] that 'Kauṭilya must have been acquainted with the whole body of *Dharmaśāstra* literature, much as we now have it, from the earliest *Dharmasūtra* down to the most recent metrical *Smṛtis* and *Smṛti* fragments'. Thus Jolly thinks that the *Arthaśāstra* is later than these *Dharmaśāstras*, not only later than the *Baudhāyana Dharmasūtra* (passage 7) which in fact is accepted even by Indian scholars, not only later than the *Manusmṛti* (Passages 8,18,20), which even Bühler considers to be possibly earlier than the Christian era[178], not only later than the *Viṣṇudharmasūtra* (passages 16,28—which Jolly thinks is earlier than the *Yājñavalkyasmṛti*)[179], but also later than *Yājñavalkya* (20 passages in all), *Nārada* (Passages 2,27), *Bṛhaspati* (Passage 1), *Kātyāyana* (Passage 5) and *Vyāsa* (Passage 3) *Smṛtis.* It must be mentioned here that Indian scholars generally think that all these *Dharmaśāstras,* except *Baudhāyana,* have borrowed from the *Arthaśāstra,* rather than the contrary. What is surprising (and a fact pointing out the way in which Jolly tries to twist arguments in his favour) is that in his Introduction to the *Nārada* and *Bṛhaspati Smṛtis,* he puts the date of the former as fifth century AD at the earliest and the sixth century at the latest,[180] and of the latter as not later than the sixth or seventh century AD[181] (i.e. later than the *Arthaśāstra* even if the *Arthaśāstra* is considered to belong to third century AD). In his introduction to his edition of the *Arthaśāstra* he makes an about-turn, and expresses the view that 'The estimates of Yājñavalkya vary and it is not certain whether the mention of Greek astrology and Greek coins in them justifies assigning them to the fourth or fifth centuries AD'.[182] It is another matter if the writer happens to agree with the last argument of Jolly that the mention of astrology or *dināra* is no criterion for fixing dates; but the manner in which he has tried to prove that *Arthaśāstra* was composed later than *Yājñavalkya* or *Nārada* is unconvincing as Jolly's statement about them are self-contradictory.

(*iv*) As regards the two *ślokas* in the *Arthaśāstra* which speak of the merits of laying down one's life in war[183], they are introduced by the words, *apīha ślokau bhavataḥ.* 'Moreover there are two stanzas in this connection and they end with the word *iti.*' It shows they are no doubt quotations. One of them is found in the *Parāśārasmṛti*[184] and the other in the *Pratijñā-Yaugandharāyaṇa* of Bhāsa.[185] As the latter verse in Bhāsa's play is also introduced by the *gātrasevaka's* words *śravantu atra bhavantaḥ,* it also seems to be a quotation in *Pratijñā-Yaugandharāyaṇa.* As it is a quotation at both places it may have been taken by both from somewhere else. It cannot therefore be used for deciding dates. Or, otherwise, it may well be, as urged by both Kane[186] and Sten Konow[187], that Bhāsa may well have borrowed it from the *Arthaśāstra*. With regard to the verse found in the *Parāśarasmṛti*, Kane places the *Smṛti* between the first and fifth century AD[188] mainly on the ground that 'it seems to have known a work of Manu'. But if Manu's date (between the second century BC and the second century AD)[189] be questionable[190] then *Parāśarasmṛti* may be of a period earlier than the third century BC and the *Arthaśāstra* may then have borrowed it from that *Smṛti*, and may be far earlier than third century AD.

As for those works which are considered to be later than the *Arthaśāstra*, Winternitz says: 'In case the *Tantrākhyāyikā* and the *Nyāyabhāṣya* could with tolerable probability be placed in the fourth century AD, the *Kauṭilīya* might possibly have been just a little older. Even the mention of the *Nandisūtra* and *Anuyogadvāra* of the Jaina canons does not go to prove anything in addition.'[191] The dates of these works, including the *Nandisūtra* and *Anuyogadvāra*, may now be considered.

(*v*) There is difference of opinion about the date of the *Tantrākhyāyikā*. Hertel, who has edited the work, puts it at about AD 300. Jolly objects to Hertel's date[192]: 'This is perhaps too early by a century or so, since that collection of tales was not translated into Pahlavi till about AD 570 and is not likely to have been composed long before that time, considering its close agreement with the Pahlavi translation'. What Jolly says amounts to this that Bühler translated the *Manusmṛti* from Sanskrit into English in 1880s and that translation closely agrees with the original. Therefore, the *Manusmṛti* must have been composed earliest in the seventeenth century AD. Such sweeping statements without any solid base have little value. But if Hertel's date of the *Tantrākhyāyikā* is accepted, that work which contains, according to Jolly, at least '30 texts derived from the *Arthaśāstra*' then the *Arthaśāstra* must have been written much earlier, i.e. earlier than the third century AD.

(*vi*) Jolly himself says that the *Nandisūtra* and *Anuyoga-dvārasūtra* are of 'uncertain date'.[193] However, it seems that mainly regarding these two, which are works of Jaina canon, though Keith has placed them in the fifth century AD,[194] Winternitz says,[195] 'That this list[196] goes back to some pre-Christian period has been proved neither by Jacobi (ZDMG71, 254f), nor by Charpentier (Uttarādhyayana Ed., Intro. p. 2f.). Even if portions of the Jaina canons go back to the Nandas, we do not have any evidence that may enable us to consider the relevant passages to be older than the age of Devarḍdhi's (fifth century AD)'. This statement of Winternitz shows that these two works may belong to a sufficiently early period, i.e. at least they may be of the pre-Christian era on the basis of Jacobi and Charpentier, but Winternitz, simply on grounds of negative arguments, assigned the relevant passages to the fifth century AD.

(*vii*) Regarding Vātsyāyana's *Kāmasūtra* (and for dating purposes the *Nyāyabhāṣya* of Vātsyāyana may be put together with it) Jolly says, 'It is here quite clear that its author has borrowed from the *Arthaśāstra* both the plan and scope of his own work and many peculiar terms as well as entire paragraphs'.[197] After enumerating various similarities between the two treatises he concludes, 'Indeed all things considered there can hardly be any doubt not only that the *Kāmasūtra* was deeply influenced by the *Arthaśāstra*, but that no long interval of time can have passed between the composition of two such cognate productions'.[198] 'If then the fourth century AD be taken as the probable date of the *Kāmasūtra* the *Arthaśāstra* may have been composed in the third century.'[199] Now, whereas Jolly gives no reason why 'no long interval of time can have passed' between these similar works, Jacobi[200] 'refers the *Arthaśāstra* to a much earlier date than *Kāmasūtra* (five or six centuries earlier)' and gives his reasons for doing so. While denying two of Jacobi's three arguments, Jolly seems to be contradicting himself. Jacobi's one reason for thinking the *Arthaśāstra* to be composed earlier than *Kāmasūtra* by several centuries is the latter's allusion to astrology (which for the Western writers ordinarily means astrology borrowed by Indians from the Greeks), while the *Arthaśāstra* does not speak of astrology. Jolly, arguing against Jacobi, i.e. trying to prove that Kauṭilya believes in astrology, says that two planets, Jupiter and Venus, are mentioned by Kauṭilya.[201] Jolly, however, as opposed to his stand here, elsewhere denies that *Arthaśāstra* believes in astrology, and says[202] that whereas Yājñavalkya recommends the worship of planets as the rise and fall of kings is dependent on them[203], the *Arthaśāstra* deplores the tendency to consult the stars too much.[204] Thus Jolly speaks in contradictory voices at two different places. The second argument of Jacobi is that the *Kāmasūtra* knows Vaiśeṣika philosophy,[205] but the *Arthaśāstra* ignores it.[206] Jolly rejects this argument on the ground that this is *argumentum ex silentio* and Kauṭilya might have known the Vaiśeṣika. But Jolly has himself used such *argumentum ex silentio*, particularly where he denies the existence of Kauṭilya.[207] So Jolly has no grounds for proving his contention that the composition date of *Kāmasūtra* is only a century later than that of the *Arthaśāstra*. It would have been better if in reply to Jacobi's arguments Jolly had accepted the fact that Vātsyāyana and Kauṭilya are identical as stated in the *Vaijayantī* of Yādavaprakāśa and the *Abhidhānacintāmaṇi* of Hemacandra. Let us quote them. The former says:

Vātsyāyano Mallanāgaḥ Kauṭilyaścaṇakātmajaḥ,
Drāmilaḥ Pakṣilasvāmī Viṣṇugupto'ṅgulaśca yaḥ.

The latter has the same names except one, Varāṇaka instead of Caṇakātmajaḥ (though in a different order):

Vātsyanastu Kauṭilyo Viṣṇugupto Varāṇakaḥ,
Drāmilaḥ Pakṣilasvāmī Mallanāgo'ṅgulo'pi ca.

The *Nāmamālika* of Bhojarāja, which seems to have the same verse as Hemacandra's has one line before that *śloka* and that is *Kātyāyano Vararuchir Mayajicca Punarvasuḥ.* Thereafter follows a *śloka* similar to Hemacandra's

Kātyāyanastu Kauṭilyo Viṣṇugupto Varaṇakaḥ,
Drāvilaḥ Pakṣilasvāmī Mallanāgo'ṅgulo'pi ca.

It seems that Kātyāyana of the previous line has been wrongly repeated in the first line of the next *śloka* and the scribe has erred in having the latter Kātyāyana instead of Vātsyāyana. Thus, according to all these three writers, Vātsyāyana is the same person as Kauṭilya, and the close similarity of *Kāmasūtra* of Vātsyāyana and the *Arthaśāstra* of Kauṭilya proves this point. Therefore, Vātsyāyana's date (either as his name is synonymous with that of Kauṭilya because of what the three dictionaries say and because of the close similarity of the two works, or as he is five or six centuries later than Kauṭilya because of what has been stated by Jacobi) as put forward by Jolly is wrong, and so the *Arthaśāstra,* in either case, belongs to the fourth century BC.

Of other works, the argument has been put forward by Trautmann[208] and, inferentially by Keith, Winternitz and Jolly,[209] that 'no work antedating the Christian era mentions Kauṭilya as the author of or unmistakenly quotes from the *Arthaśāstra;* indeed the earliest such works (the

Pañcatantra and Āryasūra's *Jātakamālā)* are probably of the Gupta period or at most just previous'.[210] What matters, however, is not whether they are prior to the Christian era or not, but whether they are post-third century AD or not because if a work of the first century AD or even of the third century AD mentions *Arthaśāstra,* the third century AD date of that book becomes doubtful. In this matter, the *Kāmasūtra,* the *Tantrākhyāyikā,* the *Nandisūtra* and the *Anuyogadvārasūtra* have already been considered.

(*viii*) Regarding *Mudrārākṣasa's* date Jolly himself is very sceptical (fifth century AD[211]).

(*ix*) Kalidāsa, according to tradition, was one of the gems of the court of the famous Vikramāditya, the founder of the Vikrama era, i.e. the first century BC (because of whom several of the later kings took pride in calling themselves Vikramādityas), and the tradition ought to be ordinarily respected unless there are very weighty reasons for not doing so.

(*x*)Both Jolly[212] and Keith[213] seem to have considered that the *Carakasaṁhitā* was composed later than the *Arthaśāstra* as the *Saṁhitā* mentions 35 *tantrayuktis* as compared to 32 in the *Arthaśāstra* (they do not mention any date of the treatise). S.N. Srivastava in his book *The Philosophical Background of the Carakasaṁhitā*[214] has placed it at 500 BC mainly on the ground of its relation to different philosophical systems. The *Carakasaṁitā* does not accept the 25 *tattvas* of Īśvarakṛṣṇa, but it does the 24 *tattvas* of the *Mahābhārata* and so, according to Dr Srivastava, it is older than the *Sāṁkhya*. The *'nitya'* of the *Carakasaṁitā*[215] is borrowed from the *nitya* of the Vaiśeṣika, and Vaiśeṣika, according to Radhakrishnan, belongs to the sixth or fifth century BC. The *Carakasaṁhitā* antedates the *Nyāyasūtra* as the *Nyāya* of the *Saṁhitā* is less developed than the *Nyāya* of the *Sūtras* and *Nyāyasutras,* according to Radhakrishnan, belong to 300 BC. On all these grounds (and other grounds also) Dr Srivastava says that the *Carakasaṁitā* was composed in *c.* 500 BC.

(*xi*) Jolly makes sweeping statements about the *Kāmandakīya Nītisāra* also. He says:[216] 'It is hardly safe to adopt the opinion of R. Mitra in his edition of the work that the Hindus in the island of Bali imported the *Nītisāra* into Bali as early as the fourth century AD. The importation may have taken place at a much later period than that'. Jolly here does not state any reasons for his opinion that the *Nītisāra* was imported into Bali much later. Perhaps the only reason behind it is that it does not suit him. Keith, however, holds that the *Nītisāra's* 'presence into the island of Bali in the Kawi literature is of no importance, as it was not till the tenth century that that literature flourished to the greatest extent'.[217] But what is important in this context is not the flourishing of that literature but its origin, for if it had originated in early fourth century, that would mean that the *Nītisāra* could have been imported there by that date. Jolly gives two reasons for the eighth century AD date of the *Nītisara.* One is a non-mention argument, that this 'work is nowhere alluded to by the authors of the earliest versions of the *Pañcatantra* nor by the ancient commentators of Manu',[218] which, as has already been emphasized, are arguments of little importance as they prove nothing. For instance, as accepted by Jolly, the *Hitopadeśa* quotes Kāmandaka, but does not mention the *Arthaśāstra.* This does not, however, prove that the *Arthaśāstra* did not exist at the time of *Hitopadeśa.*

Jolly's second argument is that Kāmandaka is once quoted by Vāmana (AD 800) and this fact has also been referred to by both Keith[219] and Winternitz.[220] On this basis all of them think that Kāmandaka belonged to the eighth century AD. On the other hand, it is on this ground alone that Kane (from whom Jolly borrows this fact)[221] assigns Kāmandaka to a much earlier period. According to Kane, Vāmana in his *Kāvyālaṅkārasūtra* quotes half a verse as an example of *yamaka—kāmaṃ Kāmandakīnītirasyā rasyā divāniśam.* ('The *dhi* indeed day and night enjoys the reading of Kāmandakī nīti').[222] Kane points out that Vāmana did not quote Kāmandaka, as Vāmana says at another place that a work called the *Hariprabhoda* treats Yamakas at length. Vāmana probably quotcd from that work. The quotation in Vāmana shows that the *Kāmandakīya Nītisāra* must have become very popular for study by the time the work (probably *Hariprabodha*) was written. All this may have taken a long period of time, may be centuries according to Kane. Kane, because of all this, concludes: 'There is nothing to prevent us from holding that the *Nītisāra* of Kāmandaka belongs to the 3rd century AD'.[223] Not only this, in the *Mahābhārata* there is a dialogue between Kāmandaka and King Aṅgariṣṭa[224] thus indicating probably an early date for Kāmandaka.

Regarding the date of the *Nītisāra,* Winternitz has another argument, a negative one, that Daṇḍin (*Daśakumāracarita*) did not know the *Nītisāra,*[225] though in a footnote[226] he accepts that Kāmandaka is mentioned at the beginning of the *Daśakumāracarita*. But, he says, the *pūrvapīṭhikā* was added later. It is difficult to accept this fact as the *Pūrvapīṭhikā* is the basis of this whole novel without which its various portions will fall apart. Thus, if both Kāmandaka and the *Tantrākhyāyikā* belong to the third century AD or earlier (as Hertel and Kane think), the *Arthaśāstra* is bound to be of a much earlier date.

Apart from these dates of composition of the various works mentioned and discussed above, only two other points are mentioned by Keith, Winternitz and Jolly in support of their thinking that the *Arthaśāstra* was composed in the third century AD. One of them is the use of the word *suruṅga*, equated by them, as said earlier, with the Greek word *syrinx*. This argument advanced, for proving that date, is advocated only by Keith[227]. He says that the word *suruṅga* was doubtless borrowed from the Greek *syrinx* 'probably not until after the Christian era'. But as the Greek word occurs for the first time in Polybius in 150 BC, therefore, even if it is originally Greek, it cannot possibly be taken to prove the third century date of the *Arthaśāstra*. This shows at the most that the *Arthaśāstra* did not exist in the fourth century BC and this point has already been dealt with earlier (p. 33–34 above).

The second point is that the knowledge of alchemy, which they say was borrowed in India from Greece in the first century AD is employed by all the three writers to prove that date. It is Jolly who had originally advanced this argument[228], and both Keith[229] and Winternitz[230] borrowed it from him. Alchemy means the process of transmuting baser metals into gold through the use of mercury.[231] But in one *sūtra*,[232] where the word *rasa* is first used,[233] it only means liquid. Here Kauṭilya refers to *bhūmiprastararasadhātu* (i.e. ores found in the earth, in rocks and in liquid form). Now, here *rasadhātu* cannot in any case be translated as mercury ores, and in the next *sūtra* (II.12.2) Jolly himself translates the word *rasa* as liquid, i.e. *rasāḥ kāñcanikāḥ* as 'liquids containing gold' not as mercury containing gold. But Jolly has tried to distort the argument in his favour, and so, in a third *sūtra*, where different types of gold are mentioned, he translates *rasa* as mercury[234] and *rasaviddha* as gold obtained by amalgamation with mercury, because he had somehow to try to introduce the process of alchemy here. Kangle, on the other hand, in that *sūtra* (in accordance with *sūtras* II.12.1 and 2 where Jolly himself has translated the word *rasa* as liquid) translates it as 'gold transmuted by means of liquid'. In II.12.2 are mentioned the gold-bearing liquids, and in II.12.3 is described the process whereby 'they (i.e. the gold-bearing liquids) are capable of transmuting copper and silver up to one-hundred times (their own weight)'. So the process of transmutation is there, but not of transmutation through the use of mercury, but through the use of gold-bearing liquids. This sort of gold is referred to in II.13.3 where various types of gold are mentioned and among them are 'gold found in a natural condition, that transmuted by means of liquids and that produced from the mines'. But Jolly, for his own purpose, translates it not as 'gold transmuted by means of liquids' but as 'gold obtained by amalgamation of mercury'. Not only this, he says: 'Regarding the age of origin of Indian alchemy, the opinion of those does not deserve much credit who believe it to have been the outcome of Indian intellectual activity'. In the footnote he refers to P.C. Roy's *History of Hindu Chemistry*. The reasons for disbelieving Roy are two. One is the dubious 'similarity with European methods' of Indian methods. This similarity is exploded once it is understood that *rasa* does not mean mercury. The other reason is the reference to Rūma (Rome), and Phiraṅgas (France) and *mlecchas* (barbarians) in Sanskrit texts on alchemy. But these references do not mean anything unless it is specifically stated that the methods of alchemy are borrowed by the Indians from these people.

On re-reading what has been said above, one finds that the dates of the *Smṛtis* (particularly the *Nārada, Bṛhaspati* and *Kātyāyana Smṛtis*), the *Tantrākhyāyikā*, the *Kāmasūtra* and the *Kāmandakīya* have been wrongly given so that these do not support the third century AD date for the *Arthaśāstra*, and wrong conclusions seem to have been drawn from the mention of the *Mahābhārata*, the *Mahābhāṣya* of

Patañjali and the *Pratijñā Yaugandharāyaṇa*. Apart from this, it has not been proved that the knowledge of alchemy was borrowed from the Greeks. Therefore, the third century AD date for the *Arthaśāstra,* which Keith, Winternitz and Jolly tried to advance, cannot be accepted.

According to B.M. Barua, the *Arthaśāstra* was composed near the beginning of the Christian era.[235] Pran Nath assigns the date as AD 484-510,[236] V.I. Kalyanov as the third century AD, and E.H. Johnstone as AD 150. These writers have not however received much acceptance, so we are not going to deal with their opinions here.

Of these three scholars, Keith and Jolly are themselves doubtful about the correctness of their dates. Keith says that the date is plausible though it cannot be proved.[237] Jolly, like Max Müller in the case of Vedic dating, thinks that this 'date, of course, is not final, but may be used as a working hypothesis'.[238] Trautmann's argument that the ancient Indian works which mentioned Kauṭilya or the *Arthaśāstra,* or those which quoted from it do not belong to the pre-Christian era, and that they may even be post-Guptan, does not cut much ice, as these works have unanimously recorded the contemporaneity of Cānakya or Viṣṇugupta or Kauṭilya and of Candragupta Maurya, and if these Western writers accept the fourth century BC date of Candragupta, they will have to accede to the same date for Kauṭilya as well. Even if these ancient Indian works mentioning Kauṭilya were composed after the third century AD (which is difficult to accept), they were in any case much nearer in time to the period of Cāṇakya and Candragupta than these twentieth century scholars, and so they can be expected to have a better knowledge about Cāṇakya (Kauṭilya) and Candragupta through oral transmissions from one generation to another, than these scholars whose contentions are based on mere conjectures.

Not only have they failed to establish the points about the date, but their efforts to do so are hardly above suspicion. All dates of composition of ancient Indian works and historical events must be carefully judged keeping in mind the Indian tradition, which should be accepted as far as possible, and any revision must be based on firm grounds. Jacobi, one of the discerning Western scholars (there are others also) says, 'Without weighty grounds one must not push aside the unanimous Indian tradition; else one practices scepticism, not criticism'.[239]

In spite of what has been said above, it is difficult to deny two facts mentioned by the above-mentioned Western writers. One is that Megasthenes, or any other Greek writer, even though they speak of Sandrakottos, do not mention Kauṭilya. The conclusion drawn from this by these writers is that either Kauṭilya is a myth, or else he did not belong to the time of Candragupta Maurya, i.e. fourth century BC. This conclusion is obviously wrong. All references to Cāṇakya and Candragupta Maurya in the Indian tradition is consistent about the fact that Cāṇakya guided Candragupta Maurya in dethroning the Nandas, obtained the crown for him and also made efforts to consolidate his rule. Kauṭilya cannot therefore be assigned a date later than the fourth century BC and if Kauṭilya did not exist at the time of Sandrakottos, as the Western writers claim, then the only valid conclusion, in view of the tradition unanimously accepted by Indian sources, can be that Sandrakottos is not Candragupta Maurya, for otherwise the Greek writers would not have failed to mention Cāṇakya or Viṣṇugupta (Kauṭilya) in connection with Sandrakottos. Now the question arises, if Sandrakottos was not Candragupta Maurya, who could he be? If the similarity of names is any guide, he might have been some other Candragupta, may be one of the two Candraguptas of the Gupta dynasty, and accounts of some of the Gupta kings (the first three kings) found elsewhere other than in Greek writings, tally[240] with the accounts of Sandrakottos mentioned by the Greeks.[241] In that case, Candragupta Maurya and Kauṭilya may have to be taken back seven centuries, i.e. near about 1000 BC. But if there are objections to equating Sandrakottos with the Gupta rulers, efforts will have to be made to find out who Sandrakottos really was. This much can, of course, be certainly said that, in any case, Candragupta Maurya and Kauṭilya may have to be pushed back by several centuries, if not seven centuries. To try to find the support for this fact in the Vedic literature would be futile because the dates of Vedic works themselves need revision as has been established in the article referred to above.

The second point mentioned by these Western scholars, particularly by Jolly,[242] which is unexceptionable, is that, if not the other *Smṛtis*, at least *Manusmṛti* existed before the *Kauṭilīya Arthaśāstra* was composed. But Jolly's motive in establishing this point, which has already been controverted, was to bring forward the date of composition of *Kauṭilīya* to the third century AD. We have already discussed some sweeping statements made by Jolly in an effort to support his contention of a later composition date for the *Arthaśāstra*.

That the *Manusmṛti* is older than the *Arthaśāstra* is indicated by one other very important reason: this is that the *Manusmṛti* speaks only of Āryāvarta, situated between the Himalayas and the Vindhyas[243], whereas the *Arthaśāstra* mentions the *Cakravartikṣetra* between the Himalayas and the seas.[244] It is strange that no scholar, either Western or Indian, has even referred to this point in connection with the dating of the *Smṛti*, though even Bühler, who has pointed out a large number of passages of the *Manusmṛti* as spurious[245], does not include this passage at all in the list of those passages which have been added later. The reason why Western scholars have not done so seems to be quite clear. This fact itself would have pushed back the *Manusmṛti*, not only to the pre-*Mahābhārata* times, because the *Mahābhārata* also describes the whole of Bhāratavarṣa, but to a much earlier date when the Aryan civilization had not spread to the south, and possibly it may even be earlier than some parts of the Vedic literature. But this would not have been to the liking of Max Müller and some other scholars like him. And the reason why no Indian scholar referred to this point seems to be that by the time Bühler had fixed the date of the *Manusmṛti* at between the second century BC and the second century AD, they, the Indian scholars, had already been so conditioned to adopt the Western methods of research, that they meekly accepted Bühler's date. But by the time the *Arthaśāstra* was discovered, Indian scholarship had emerged in its own right, and attempts by Western scholarship to push back the date of that work to the third century AD were very strongly challenged. Having earlier accepted the date of the *Manusmṛti* between the second century BC and the second century AD and of the *Arthaśāstra* as of the fourth century BC, Indian scholarship tried in every possible way to prove that the date of composition of the *smṛti* was later than that of the *Arthaśāstra.* One very senior Indian scholar told me that there should be no attempt to prove that the *Manusmṛti* was older than the *Kauṭilīya Arthaśāstra* as that might lead to the misconception that the *Arthaśāstra* belonged to the third century AD. This is one of the reasons (but not the only one) for writing this essay as a prelude to another one regarding the respective chronological position of the two treatises. Whatever the reason for the Western or Indian scholars not to refer to the fact that the *Manusmṛti* was written at a time when the country was confined to the region between the Himalayas and the Vindhyas, i.e. Āryāvarta, it is certain that this ground alone (there are other grounds also) is sufficient to show that *Manusmṛti* is older than the *Kauṭilīya Arthaśāstra*, but then the date of production of the *Manusmṛti* will have to be taken back sufficiently, probably a millennium or so, though how much backwards cannot be stated with certainty. What can, however, be emphasized is that the whole Western dating (as also Indian dating which follows the former's footsteps) shall have to be revised, keeping in view, as stated above, all these ideas that are prevalent in the Indian tradition.

Basham is one of the latest of such scholars, who tried to place ancient Indian works as late as possible. He himself tried to fix the *Arthaśāstra*, as it seems, at the third century AD though ostensibly he simply said that it was post-fourth century BC. Basham also says, though in another context: 'Such patriotic scholars as Dr K.P. Jayaswal, writing when Indian independence had not been achieved, did much to give people faith in themselves, and, therefore, may have served a practical purpose.'[246] What he wanted to say further seems to be that such scholars had made a forced interpretation of facts, and that as independence has now been achieved, patriotism is not needed any more and Indians should acquiesce in what the Western writers say. If they do not do so they are proceeding on the same lines as their predecessors like Dr Jayaswal did, i.e. they are trying to make forced interpretations. It is possible that on certain matters Indian thinkers may have made strained interpretations of facts which should not have been done. But are not Western thinkers also—such as Basham and some others—guilty of obvious bias? What about the repeated assertions that Kauṭilya did not live in the fourth century BC when Candragupta Maurya is accepted to have existed then and as per Indian tradition the two worked together? This denial was based simply on some dubious proofs, which some Western scholars claim to have found (or worked up). Is not this a forced interpretation of facts? What Basham seems to want is that Indian nationalism should efface itself and let Western chauvinism have its course.

Jolted by the strong criticism made by Indian scholars of the third century AD composition date of the *Arthaśāstra*, Basham wished that that date should be proved scientifically with the help of a computer (though computer has nothing to do with scientism). He tried to inspire his students to do this job[247] and one of them, Thomas R. Trautmann, took it up, completed it through statistical analysis, and his results were published in *Kauṭilya and the Arthaśāstra*. As has already been said, this analysis (statistical) is of a different nature from the previous one made by Jolly and others. The second part of this essay is reserved for a consideration of the nature and validity of the statistical analysis.

References

[1] I.5. 16–20.
Moriyānam khattiyānaṃ vaṁsajātaṃ sirīdharaṃ /
Candagupto'ti pañjātaṃ Cāṇakko brāhamaṇo tato //
Navanaṃ Dhananandaṃ taṃ ghātetvā caṇḍakodhavā/
Sakale Jambudīpasmiṃ rajje samabhisiñcaso //

[2] VI.14–15.

[3] IV.24.26–30.
Tataścana vā caitānnandān Kauṭilyo brāhamaṇa samuddhariṣyati /
Teśāmabhāve Mauryā pṛthivīṃ bhokṣyanti //
Kauṭilya eva Candraguptamutpannaṃ rājye' bhiṣekṣyati /
Tasyāpi putro Bindusāro bhaviṣyati // tasyāpyaśokavardhanaḥ

[4] *Vāyu Purāṇa* (99.326–33) and the *Brahmāṇḍa Purāṇa* (II.3.74.141-5) give the reigning periods of the Nandas (or of their last king which is 100 years), and of Candragupta (24 years), Bhadrasāra (or Bindusāra 25 years), and Aśoka (26 years).
Brahmāṇḍa Purāṇa states:
Uddhariśyati tānsaravān Kauṭilyo vai dvijarṣabha /
Bhuktvā mahīṃ varṣaśataṃ narendraḥ sambhaviśyati //
Candraguptaṃ nṛpe rājyaṃ Kauṭilyo sthāpayiṣyati /
Caturviṁśati samā rājā Candragupto bhaviṣyati //
Bhavitā Bhadrasārastu pañcaviṁśatsamā nṛpaḥ /
ṣaḍtriṁśattu samā rājā Aśokānāṃ ca tṛptidaḥ //
The *Matsya Purāṇa* (272.22), speaks of twelve sons of Nanda but does not give the names (like the *Viṣṇu Purāṇa* and the reigning periods of the Mauryan kings); whereas the *Bhāgavata Purāṇa* says that it was a Brāhmaṇa (*dvija*, without giving his name), who destroyed the Nandas and coronated Candragupta, whose son was Bindusāra (or Vārisāra), and then his son was Aśokavardhana,XXII.1.12–13.
Matsya—Uddhariśyati Kauṭilyaḥ samairdvādāśabhiḥ sutān /
Bhuktvā mahīṃ varṣaśataṃ tato Mauryān gamiṣyati //
Bhāgavata—Navanandān dvijaḥ kaścita prapannānuddhariṣyati/
Teṣāmabhāve jagatiṃ Mauryā bhokṣyanti vai kalau //
Sa eva Candraguptaṃ vai dvijo rājye'bhiṣekṣyati /
Tatsuto Bindusārastu (Vārisārastu) tatścāśokavardhanaḥ

[5] I.6.

[6] I.4–5.

[7] Introductory story.

[8] After VII.8.

[9] V.22.

[10] I.22 and the speech just before it.

[11] Cf., R.P. Kangle, *Kauṭilīya Arthaśāstra, Part I,* University of Bombay, 1970, II.8.20–21.

[12] Cf., Ibid., V.4. 13–14, one half of each *śloka.*

[13] 2nd verse.

[14] Taken from Kane's *History of the Dharmaśāstra,* vol. I, (2nd edition), Bhandarkar Oriental Research Institute, Poona, 1968, p. 181, note 166.

[15] I.1.20.

[16] *Kauṭilīya Arthaśāstra: A Study,* part-III, Bombay, 1965, p. 61.

[17] Kangle also holds that the *śloka* (XV.1.73) and the *śloka* after the colophon at the end of the book are later additions, and though he seems to accept the tradition that 'Kauṭilya is the author of this text' (p. 60), yet on the basis of his above-mentioned opinion regarding the passages cited, he feels that the evidence of this tradition cannot be accepted as decisive. Yet, in spite of this doubt Kangle later on (pp. 61–77) strongly refutes the arguments of the writers who doubt the existence of Kauṭilya and of the genuineness of his being the author of the *Arthaśāstra.* In any case it is necessary to go into the arguments of Kangle as regards the supposed interpolations.

[18] Ibid., p. 21.

[19] Ibid., pp. 20–21.

[20] The word '*śāstra*' has been used in the sense of a written work or treatise not only here, but also in I.1.1. (*idamarthaśāstraṃ kṛtaṃ*), in I.1.19 (*Kauṭilyena kṛtaṃ śāstraṃ*), XV, 1, 73 (*śāstramidaṃ kṛtaṃ*) and also in the verse at the end of the colophon. In this (II.10.63) *śloka* Kauṭilya seems to refer to the works of his predecessors because all the sciences here cannot mean sciences other than '*rājanīti*' or '*nītiśāstra*'.

[21] *History of Dharmaśāstra,* vol. 1, 2nd edition, p. 175, f.n. 163.

[22] The word '*śāstra*' in the first line of this verse means the science of politics, and in the second line it refers to this particular work.

[23] *Kauṭilīya Arthaśāstra: A Study,* part III, p. 61.

[24] The f.n. to this *śloka* in the translation of the *Arthaśāstra,* Bombay, 1972.

[25] T.R. Trautmann, *Kauṭilya and the Arthaśāstra,* E.J. Brill, Leiden, 1971, p. 5.

[26] ZDMG, 68, 1914, 369 referred to in M. Winternitz's *History of Indian Literature,* vol. III, part-II, tr. Subhadra Jha, reprint, Motilal Banarsidass, Delhi, 1963, p. 589, f.n.1.

[27] *Megasthenes und Kauṭilya,* Wien, 1921.

[28] Introduction to his edition of the *Arthaśāstra,* Motilal Banarsidass, Lahore, 1923.

[29] Calcutta Review, April–June 1924.

[30] A.B. Keith, *History of Sanskrit Literature,* Oxford University Press, Oxford, 1928, p. 459; M. Winternitz, *History of Indian Literature,* tr. Subhadra Jha, vol. III, part 2, p. 589, reprint Motilal Banarsidass.

Henceforth, these books shall be referred to as ABK and MW respectively.

[31] *Proceedings of the First Oriental Conference*, Poona, 1919, pp. 24–25.

[32] MW, p. 590; ABK, p. 460.

[33] MW, p. 590; ABK, p. 459; Thomas R. Trautmann, *Kauṭilya and the Arthaśāstra*, p. 5. Henceforth, this book shall be referred to as TRT.

[34] *Kauṭilīya Arthaśāstra—A Study*, part III, p. 63.

[35] MW, p. 590.

[36] Junius Jolly, Introduction to his edition of the *Arthaśāstra*, op. cit., p. 34. Henceforth, this Introduction will be referred to as JJ.

[37] *History of Ancient Sanskrit Literature*, reprint, Motilal Banarsidass, Delhi, 1963, pp. 217–18, pp. 394–5, where Max Müller calls his ideas 'merely conjectural'; also see his Introduction to *Ṛg Veda*, vol. IV, pp. XIV–XV.

[38] MW, p. 589.

[39] Ibid., p. 590.

[40] MW, p. 591

[41] ABK, p. 459.

[42] Ibid.

[43] MW, pp. 590–91.

[44] MW, p. 591.

[45] JJ, p. 44.

[46] *History of Dharmaśāstra*, vol. I, pp.167, 187, 191, 196.

[47] JJ, p. 44.

[48] JJ, p. 45

[49] *Kauṭilīya Arthaśāstra*, II.11.28

[50] Ibid., VII. 12.22–24.

[51] Ibid., pp. 16–17 above, f.n. 34.

[52] ABK, p. 459.

[53] p. 19 above.

[54] Uber das, *Kauṭilyaśāstra und Verwandtes* p. 10. Reference taken from Kangle's *Kauṭilīya Arthaśāstra: A Study*, part III, pp. 101–5.

[55] ABK, p. 459.

[56] MW, p. 591.

[57] *History of Dharmaśāstra*, vol. I, pp. 195, 209.

[58] XV. 1.21–22.

[59] I.15.47–50.

[60] JJ, p. 45.

[61] ABK, p. 459.

[62] MW, p. 591.

[63] JJ, p. 43.

[64] *Arthaśāstra*, II. 11.28.

[65] Ibid., VII. 12.22–24.

[66] JJ, p. 44.

[67] *Arthaśāstra*, II.30.29. For explanation, see footnote to the translation.
[68] Ibid., II.11.37. See notes to the translation.
[69] Ibid., II.11.69.
[70] Ibid., II.12.102.
[71] Ibid., II.11.42.
[72] Ibid., II.11.107.
[73] Ibid., VII.12.26
[74] MW, p. 592.
[75] JJ, p. 45.
[76] JJ, p. 44.
[77] For the statements in the *Daśakumāracarita*, see pp.5, 7–8 and *Pañcatantra*, see pp. 8–9 above.
[78] For statements in *Tantrākhyāyikā*, see p.10 above.
[79] *Kadambari-Kiṃ vā teṣāṃ sāmprataṃ yeṣāmatinṛśaṁsaprāyopadeśa nirghṛaṇaṃ Kauṭilyaśāstraṃ pramāṇaṃ abhicārakriyākaraikaṃ prakṛtayaḥ purodhaso guruvaḥ parābhisandhānaparā mantriṇaḥ updeṣṭāraḥ narapatisahasrojjhitāyāṃ lakṣmyāmāsaktiḥ māraṇātmakeṣu śāstreṣvabhiyogaḥ sahajapremādrahṛdayānuruktā bhrātara ucchedyāḥ*
[80] *Khameamaccaputte cānakkai caiva thūlavaddeyaṃ* and *Bhārahaṃ Rāmāyaṇaṃ Bhīmāsurakkaṃ Kauḍilliyaṃ*
[81] I.2–6.
[82] See p. 19–22, (b) point (ii) above.
[83] JJ, pp. 38–40.
[84] For Stein see *The Kauṭilīya Arthaśāstra: A Study*, part III, p. 68.
[85] The *Arthaśāstra* is a theoretical work and the practice in Candragupta Maurya's reign to which Jolly refers may have been the same as written by Megasthenes. The writer stayed for some time in Udaipur, one of the divisional centres in Rajasthan. What he strangely found there in 1958 was that, though there were laws against theft, robbery and molestation of women, in the city itself there were no thefts in houses, and that things left unguarded in the streets would not be picked up by anyone. In the rural areas of Udaipur women laden up with ornaments could pass any area without fear of any kind of molestation. (Things may have now become different under the influence of the industrial civilization and the deteriorating law and order situation in present times). So it is possible that Megasthenes may have depicted the conditions as they existed in Candragupta's reign and not idealistic ideas.
[86] JJ, p. 35.
[87] *History of Dharmaśāstra*, vol. I, p. 194.
[88] Bühler, Introduction to trans. of *Vasiṣṭha Dharmasūtra*, reprint Motilal Banarsidass, Delhi, 1975, p. xxvi.

[89] Ibid.
[90] *Kauṭilīya Arthaśāstra: A Study*, part III, p. 91.
[91] *Arthaśāstra*, II.10.1–2
[92] Ibid., I.9.3
[93] Ibid., II.10.38–46.
[94] *Indian Antiquary*, vol. LIII, 1924, pp. 128–36, esp. 133–36.
[95] JJ, p. 35; Also ABK, p. 460.
[96] *Arthaśāstra*, II.12.22 and 28.
[97] McCrindle, *Ancient India as Described by Megasthenes and Arrian*, Bombay, 1877, p. 30.
[98] Ibid., p.251
[99] Rostovtzeff, *The Social and Political History of the Hellenistic Period*, Oxford, 1941, p. 1218. Reference from Kangle, *The Kauṭilīya Arthaśāstra*, part III, p. 71.
[100] JJ, p. 35; ABK, p. 460.
[101] M. Winternitz, *Some Problems of Indian Literature*, Calcutta, 1925, pp. 100 ff.
[102] *Kauṭilīya Arthaśāstra*, II.6.1-3; II.15.1-11; II.12, 26, 28, 30–36.
[103] S.N. Mital, 'Taxation in the *Kauṭilīya Arthaśāstra*', in *Annals of Bhandarkar Oriental Research Institute*, 1995, pp. 69–76; also see pp. 76–87.
[104] *Kauṭilīya Arthaśāstra*, II.6.2–3,10; II.15.1.
[105] Ibid., II.26.3.
[106] Ibid., II.22.1–3; II.21.31.
[107] Ibid., II.25.40.
[108] Ibid., II.22. 3–7.
[109] Ibid., I.13.6.
[110] Ibid., II.5.8.
[111] Ibid., II.19.42; II.26, 12, 28, 30–31.
[112] Ibid., II.12, 24, 29.
[113] Ibid., II.28.25; II.34.12; II.16.18; II.29.7.
[114] Ibid., II.24.18.
[115] Ibid., II.26.3.
[116] Ibid., II.25.39.
[117] Ibid., II.27.26.
[118] VIII.307.
[119] JJ, p. 35.
[120] ZII, vol. III, pp. 280 ff. Also referred to in ABK, p. 460.
[121] ABK, p. 460.
[122] ABK, p. 460; J., p. 34.
[123] *The Greeks in Bactria and India*, p. 307.
[124] *Kauṭilīya Arthaśāstra: A Study*, part III, p. 76.
[125] *Kauṭilya and the Arthaśāstra*, Leiden, 1971, p .5.
[126] 'On Aryan Problem — fifty years later', in *Antiquity*, vol. I, 1927, pp. 204–15.

[127] 'Early Commerce of Babylon with India', in JRAS, 1896, pp. 241–73.
[128] L.R. Farnell, in *Greece and Babylon*, p. 46.
[129] *Pavry Commemoration Volume*, pp. 399–402.
[130] *Jātaka*, no. 339
[131] 15.1.4 and 15.1.73
[132] Hulzsch (ed.), *Corpus Inscriptionum Indicarum*, vol. I, pp. 48, 87.
[133] The five king were alive in 258 BC. References on ancient India's contact with West are from Kane, *History of Dharmaśāstra*, vol. V, 1958, pp. 598–600
[134] N.B. Utgikar, tr., *Indian Antiquary*, vol. LIII, 1924, p. 133
[135] This single (treatise on the) Science of Politics has been prepared by bringing together (the teaching of) as many treatises on the Science of Politics as have been composed by ancient teachers for the acquisition and protection of the earth.
[136] JJ, Introduction to his edition of *Arthaśāstra*, p. 35.
[137] MW, p. 592.
[138] ABK, pp. 461–62."The theory that the information given in the text was merely derived from fellow experts is contradicted by the express assertion of the text and all probability."
[139] JJ, p. 33.
[140] See for example, *Gautama Dharmasūtra*, ch. XI.
[141] JJ, p. 30.
[142] See 'Dating of the *Manusmṛti*', in *Journal of the Oriental Institute*, vol. XLIII, nos. 3–4, March–June 1994, pp. 167–94.
[143] *Kauṭilīya Arthaśāstra*, I.1.1.
[144] *Kāmandakīya Nitisāra*, I.6.
[145] JJ, p. 20.
[146] JJ, p. 21.
[147] Chapter 59.
[148] I.1.
[149] III.21; III.25; IX.2.
[150] *Ṛgveda* I.25.3; *Atharvaveda* IV.16.4; V.63.
[151] X.173.
[152] See Spellman, *Political Theory of Ancient India;* Kane, *History of Dharmaśāstra*, vol. III, pp. 1–234.
[153] *Bṛhadāraṇyaka Upaniṣad*, VI.4.1–4.
[154] *Chāndogya Upaniṣad*, VII.22.
[155] IV.34.
[156] I.3.14,16.
[157] E.g., I.2.9; I.17.31–33; I.19.33; III.1.41–42; III.7.30.38; XV.1.71–72.
[158] I.6.
[159] E.g., I.13.7–8; I.19.34.
[160] See the following discussion, pp. 40–41.

[161] V.1. Other chapters (e.g. I.13; XIII.5) which deal with such matters refer to this chapter ('Silent Punishment' V.1.4)
[162] *Kauṭilīya Arthaśāstra,* V.1.57.
[163] Pp. 32–33 above.
[164] Refer to article mentioned in reference no. 103 above for all these facts.
[165] *Kauṭilīya Arthaśāstra,* V.2.2–27.
[166] Ibid., V.2.30.
[167] Ibid., V.2.31–36.
[168] Ibid., V.2.70.
[169] *Arthaśāstra,* VI.1.10.
[170] Ibid., II.8.3; II.22.15; II.25.40. (Here, the word *ucita,* i.e. 'proper' has been used).
[171] Ibid., II.16.6.
[172] Ibid., I.6.7; I.13.3; II.1.15–16; II.1.37; II.9.15–16.
[173] JJ, pp. 30–31.
[174] MW, p. 593.
[175] *History of Dharmaśāstra,* vol. I, p. 366. According to Winternitz (History of Indian Literature, Vol. I, tr. Mrs. S. Ketkar, p. 465), this date (of the composition of the *Mahābhārata*) is the fourth century BC.
[176] Ibid., pp. 75–79.
[177] JJ, p. 17.
[178] Introduction to his translation of the *Manusmṛti,* S.B.E., vol. XXV, reprint, Motilal Banarsidass, Delhi, 1982, p. CXVII.
[179] Introduction to his translation of the *Viṣṇu Dharmasūtra,* pp. XX–XXII.
[180] Introduction to his translation of *Nāradasmṛti,* S.B.E., vol. XXXIII, reprint, Motilal Banarsidass, Delhi 1977, p. XVII.
[181] Introduction to his translation of *Bṛhaspatismṛti,* S.B.E., vol. XXXIII, reprint, Motilal Banarsidass, Delhi, 1970, p. 276.
[182] JJ, p. 19.
[183] *Arthaśāstra,* X.3.30–31.
[184] III.45.
[185] Act IV, s.31.
[186] *History of Dharmaśāstra,* vol. I, p. 178.
[187] *Kauṭilyan Studies,* referred to in Kane, ibid.
[188] *History of Dharmaśāstra,* vol. I, p. 464.
[189] Buhler, Introduction to his translation of the *Manusmṛti,* p. CXVII, fixed on the basis of Max Müller's opinion that the *Dharmasūtras* were written between sixth century BC and second century BC and that all metrical *smṛtis* are later than all the *Dharmasūtras.*
[190] S.N. Mital, 'Dating of *Manusmṛti*', in *Journal of Oriental Institute,* Baroda, vol. XLIII, nos. III–IV, March–June 1994, pp. 167–194.
[191] MW, p. 593.
[192] JJ, p. 8.

[193] JJ, p. 10.
[194] ABK, p. 461.
[195] MW, p. 593, f.n. 4
[196] Probably of the Jaina Canons.
[197] JJ, p. 21
[198] JJ, p. 24
[199] JJ, p. 29. Also cf. Keith, p. 493.
[200] Cf. JJ, pp. 24–26.
[201] II.24.7–8
[202] JJ, p. 4
[203] *Yājñavalkyasmṛti*, I.295–308, especially 308.
[204] *Arthaśāstra*, IX.4.26 (37 in Jolly's edition).
[205] I.2 definition of *Kāma*.
[206] I.21.10.
[207] JJ, pp. 33–34.
[208] *Kauṭilya and the Arthaśāstra*, p. 6.
[209] ABK, pp. 460–61; MW, p. 593; JJ, pp. 6–30.
[210] p. 6.
[211] JJ, p. 11.
[212] JJ, p. 9.
[213] ABK., p. 461.
[214] Pp.11–13. The thesis is in Hindi.
[215] *Śārīrasthāna*, I.59.
[216] JJ, p. 7.
[217] ABK, p. 463.
[218] JJ, p. 7.
[219] ABK, p. 463.
[220] MW, p. 597.
[221] JJ, p. 7, f.n.1.
[222] The translation is quoted from Kane referred to below.
[223] *History of Dharmaśāstra*, vol. I, p. 170.
[224] XII.123.
[225] MW., p. 597.
[226] Footnote 4.
[227] ABK, p. 460.
[228] JJ, pp. 42–43.
[229] ABK, p. 460 f.n.3.
[230] MW, p. 593, f.n.3.
[231] JJ, p. 42. Mercury is referred to as *rasa*.
[232] II.12.1.
[233] *Arthaśāstra*, II.12.1.
[234] II.13.3.

[235] 'The *Arthaśāstra*: Blend of Old and New', in *Bhāratakaumudī* (in honour of Professor R.K. Mookerji), pp. 85–119.

[236] 'The Date of the *Kauṭilīya Arthaśāstra*', in *Indian Antiquary*, vol. LX, pp. 109–12. Also refer to E.H. Johnstone, JRAS, 1929, pp. 77–81, and V.I. Kalyanov, 'Dating the *Arthaśāstra*', the paper read before the Congress of Orientalists, Cambridge 1954. These references taken from Kangle, *Kauṭilīya Arthaśāstra: A Study*, part III, pp. 96–97.

[237] ABK, p. 461.

[238] JJ, p. 29.

[239] ZDMG, 68, p. 605, quoted in Kangle, *Kauṭilīya Arthaśāstra: A Study*, part III, p. 98.

[240] Max Müller, *History of Ancient Sanskrit Literature*, reprint, Motilal Banarsidass, pp. 146–149.

[241] S.N. Mital, 'Max Müller's Vedic Dating', in *Journal of G.N. Jha Kendriya Sanskrit Vidyapeetha*, vol. XLV, pp. 63–64.

[242] JJ, pp. 37–42, also see pp. 16–24.

[243] II.17–24.

[244] IX.1.17–18.

[245] Introduction to *Manusmṛti*, SBE vol. XXV, pp. LXVII–LXXIII, Reprint Motilal Banarsidass, Delhi, 1982.

[246] *The Wonder That Was India*, p. 111.

[247] Preface to Trautmann's *Kauṭilya and the Arthaśāstra*, p. IX.

PART II

A Study of Trautmann's Statistical Analysis

The *Arthaśāstra* of Kauṭilya came to light in 1909 when it was published by Shamsastri in the Mysore Sanskrit Series. Immediately after the *Arthaśāstra* was discovered, Hillebrandt advanced the view that Kauṭilya was not the author of the whole of the *Arthaśāstra* 'though he was the founder of the school' and Hertel supported him in that the *Arthaśāstra* of Kauṭilya was worked upon and enlarged in course of time.[1] Between 1920 and 1923 various Western scholars—Winternitz,[2] Jolly,[3] Keith,[4] and Stein[5]—advanced the opinion that Kauṭilya was a work of the third century AD though they did not say anything in favour of the opinion of Hillebrandt or Hertel that the *Arthaśāstra* of Kauṭilya was a revised version of an original. Basham[6] combined the two strains. He said: 'The text refers to peoples and places (notably China) which do not seem to have been known to the Indians in the fourth century BC. It does not use much of the official terminology employed in the Aśokan inscriptions or in the Pali scriptures, but it contains many governmental terms which apparently did not become popular until post-Mauryan times.' It . . . 'is the elaboration of a Mauryan original which was perhaps the work of Kauṭilya himself'. However, Hillebrandt's and Hertel's opinions had not become popular, and the arguments in favour of the idea that the *Arthaśāstra* was a work of the third century AD were forcefully and logically refuted by a host of Indian and Western scholars.[6a] Basham, however, persisted in his opinions and definitely wanted them to be established by proof. At the University of Wisconsin he referred to his doubts before his students, as to whether the *Arthaśāstra* was 'the work of a single hand and suggested the possibility that the new technique of stylistic analysis with the aid of the computer might solve many problems concerning its date and authorship'.[7]

Trautmann, acting on Basham's advice, tried to do that. 'After six decades of scholarship there has been no general agreement on the date of the *Arthaśāstra*. . . . The only point on which there has been a large measure of agreement, tacit or express, is that the *Arthaśāstra*, though drawing on older works, has a single author.'[8] He seeks to undo that through the method suggested by Basham, and Basham has firmly supported the authenticity of Trautmann's conclusions by using strong words such as, that the method adopted by Trautmann 'appears to be virtually infallible', and that 'This is not a matter of opinion but a fact which can be established statistically and hence there is little basis for questioning Trautmann's conclusions. . . . He has proved with *something approaching certainty* that the *Arthaśāstra* is a compilation, containing the work of at least three hands'.[9] (Emphasis mine).

In the following pages a modest attempt will be made to examine Trautmann's conclusions applying the very method adopted by him.

1. Preliminary Objections

(a) Study based only on the use of *vā* (or) and *ca* (and)

Trautmann has, in his statistical method, selected 32 indeclinables[10]. This list is later reduced to five (*eva, evaṃ, ca, tatra* and *vā)*[11] as they are likely to prove 'effective discriminators'. Of these five, while testing the *Arthaśāstra*, three were found to have a 'poor discriminating ability',[12] and, therefore, the conclusions of Trautmann are based on the use of *ca* and *vā* in the different portions of the *Arthaśāstra*. The reason is that 'Most of the particles are of fairly low frequency with the brilliant exceptions of *ca* and *vā*'.[13] Actually, it would have been better if instead of the use of *ca* and *vā*, the use of some special word or words were made the basis of the determination of the authorship, whether such words were nouns or adjectives or adverbs, as has been done, according to Trautmann, by Alvar Ellegarde regarding the Junius letters. However, Trautmann does not favour that method 'because it requires large masses of texts', 'is extremely laborious', and as 'easier approaches have been found'. Therefore, Trautmann feels that 'it is the utterly mundane high frequency function words which prove the best discriminators', a conclusion he draws from Mosteller and Wallace's study of the disputed Federalist papers. He extends this conclusion, in order to justify his study, by saying that 'besides the obvious advantages that high-frequency words have in yielding a sufficient number of occurrences for statistical use from smaller samples, such words are the least affected by the subject-matter under discussion, being distributed more or less evenly from one work to another within the corpus of a single author regardless of content'.[14] We will discuss later whether the subject-matter under discussion affects the use of such words or not.[15]

(b) Counting of occurrences of *vā* and *ca* not necessary

Trautmann begins by computing the total use of some particles (eleven in all) in four samples of three Books of the *Arthaśāstra* (2, 7, 9), two samples coming from Book 2. He then gives only the *ca-vā* ratio in these samples.[16] If Trautmann had persisted with these figures and made his calculations on that basis, that would have been more justifiable, but for some inexplicable reasons he turns to examine the occurrence per sentence of these two words. Even that study could have been thought to be valid if these occurrences were found to be more or less uniform, at least in each portion, which, according to Trautmann, was written by one author. But this is not so and examples to show that this is not so are given below from Books 2, 3, 7, and 9 (because while he begins his study in the third chapter with Books 2, 7 and 9, in the fourth chapter he replaces Book 9 with Book 3 and draws his conclusions on the basis of Books 2, 3 and 7).

In Book 2, in the case of *ca* in chapter 19, whereas in 45 sentences, 41 (i.e. 8/9) have no *ca-s*, three have one *ca* each and one has two *ca-s*—in all five *ca-s*; in chapter 35, on the other hand, out of 14 sentences only two (i.e. only 1/7) have no *ca-s*, seven have one *ca* each, three have two *ca*-s each, one has three *ca-s*, and one has four *ca-s*—in all twenty *ca-s*. In the same Book, in the case of *vā*, the differences are not so great, though considerable. In chapter 20, out of 64 sentences, 61 have no *vā-s* (12/13) and the remaining three have one *vā* each—in all three *vā-s*; in chapter 14, out of 54 sentences only 32 (i.e. a little more than half only) have no *vā-s* while 18 have one *vā* each and four have two *vā-s* each—in all 26 *vā-s*, i.e. proportionately ten times more than in chapter 20.

In Book 3, in chapter 7, out of 39 sentences 34 (7/8) have no *vā-s*, and five have one *vā* each (5 *vā-s* in all); in chapter 12, out of 52 sentences only 30 (i.e. a little more than half) have no *vā-s*, while 16 have one *vā* each, 5 have two *vā-s* each and one five *vā-s* (31 *vā-s* in all—a ratio of more than 1:4 as compared with chapter 7). In this Book again, in chapter 7, as with *vā*, out of 39 sentences, 34 (7/8) have no *ca*-s and five one *ca* each (5 *ca*-s in all); in chapter 20, out of 23 sentences, only 12 (half) have no *ca*, while ten have one *ca* each and one has two *ca*-s (12 *ca*-s in all, i.e. proportionately four times more).

In Book 7, in chapter 13, out of 34 sentences, 31 have no *vā* (more than 6/7th) and three have one each (3 *vā-s* in all); in chapter 7, out of 30 sentences 15 (i.e. half) have no *vā*, five have one each, four have two each, three have three each, two have four each, and one has five *vā-s* (35 *vā-s* in all, i.e. proportionately nearly thirteen times more than in chapter 13). Again, in the same Book, calculating the figure for *ca-s*, in chapter 7, none of the 30 sentences have any *ca* at all. In chapter 16, out of 32 sentences only a little more than half (19) have no *ca*, while ten have one *ca* each and three two *ca*-s each in all 16 *ca-s*.

In Book 9, in the 1st chapter, out of 51 sentences, 46 (9/10) have no *vā-s*, four have one *vā* each and one has two *vā-s* (6 *vā-s* in all); in chapter 3, out of 41 sentences, only 19 have no *vā-s*, whereas 17 have one *vā* each, three have two *vā-s* each, one has three *vā-s* and one has seven *vā-s* (33 *vā-s* in all, proportionately four times more than in chapter 1). In this Book as regards *ca* in chapter 7, out of 83 sentences, 75 (16/17) have no *ca-s* and seven have one *ca* each and one has two *ca*-s (9 *ca-s* in all); in the 1st chapter out of 51 sentences, seven have one *ca* each, four have two *ca*-s each, two have three *ca-s*, and one has four *ca*-s (25 *ca*-s in all, proportionately four and a half times more than in chapter 7). The differences, therefore, in these four books, in two chapters each with respect to *vā* and *ca*, are not only in the total number of *vā-s* and *ca*-s in each chapter but also in one and more occurrences of the two words. As already said other chapters fall between these two extremes.

The above figures are given in a tabular form below.

In this table in the first two lines occurrences in the two chapters of each group are mentioned while in the third line are given the proportionate figures of occurrences of the second chapter in relation to the first chapter, i.e. the sentences of the latter are equated with the former to indicate the proper nature of the difference.

TABLE I

Extreme difference in occurrences of *vā* and *ca* in four Books of the *Arthaśāstra*.

Book 2 - *Vā*

Chapter	Sentences (*sūtras*)	Occurences					Total No. of particles
		0	1	2	3	3	+
20	64	61	3	0	0	0	3
14	54	32	18	4	0	0	26
		(38)	(21)	(5)	(0)	(0)	(31)

Chapter 14 has proportionately ten times more *vā*-s.

Book 2 - *Ca*

Chapter	Sentences (*sūtras*)	Occurences					Total No. of particles
		0	1	2	3	3	+
19	45	41	3	1	0	0	5
35	14	2	7	3	1	1(4)	20
		(6)	(23)	(10)	(3)	[3(4)]	(64)

Chapter 35 has proportionately thirteen times more *ca*-s.

Book 3 - *Vā*

Chapter	Sentences (*sūtras*)	Occurences					Total No. of particles
		0	1	2	3	3+	
7	39	34	5	0	0	0	5
12	52	30	16	5	0	1(5)	31
		(22)	(12)	(0)	(0)	(0)	(19)

Chapter 12 has proportionately four times more *vā-s.*

Book 3 - *Ca*

Chapter	Sentences (*sūtras*)	Occurences					Total No. of particles
		0	1	2	3	3	+
7	39	34	5	0	0	0	5
20	23	12	10	1	0	0	12
		(20)	(17)	(2)	(0)	(0)	(21)

Chapter 20 has proportionately four times more *ca-s.*

Book 7 - *Vā*

Chapter	Sentences (*sūtras*)	Occurences					Total No. of particles
		0	1	2	3	3+	
13	34	31	3	0	0	0	3
7	30	15	5	4	3	2 (4), 1(5)	35
		(17)	(6)	(5)	(3)	24	(38)

Chapter 7 has proportionately nearly thirteen times more *vā-s.*

Book 7 - *Ca*

Chapter	Sentences (*sūtras*)	Occurences					Total No. of particles
		0	1	2	3	3+	
7	30	30	0	0	0	0	0
16	32	19	10	3	0	0	16
		(35)	(0)	(0)	(0)	(0)	(0)

Chapter 16 proportionately has far more *ca-s*

Book 9 - *Vā*

Chapter	Sentences (*sūtras*)	Occurences 0	1	2	3	3+	Total No. of particles
1	51	46	4	1	0	0	6
3	41	19	17	3	1	1 (7)	33
		(24)	(21)	(4)	(1)	9 (7)	(39)

Chapter 3 has proportionately five times more *vā*-s.

Book 9 - *Ca*

Chapter	Sentences (*sūtras*)	Occurences 0	1	2	3	3+	Total No. of particles
7	83	75	7	1	0	0	9
1	51	37	7	4	2	1 (4)	25
		(60)	(11)	(7)	(3)	(7)	(41)

Chapter 1 has proportionately four times more *ca*-s.

In the above table it will be seen that within one Book the number of zero, one, two, three and more than three occurrences of both *vā* and *ca* in each of the two chapters is quite different, and other chapters in the Book falling between these two extremes.

Thus, there is so much divergence in the occurrences of *vā* and *ca* in different chapters of the same Books that it is difficult to accept that the study of occurrences per sentence can have any bearing on the issue of authorship or that conclusions drawn from such study are any better than those drawn from the total number of *vā*-s and *ca*-s in different Books. Apart from it, calculation made on the basis of occurrences does not give a correct view of the difference in the use of *vā* and *ca* in various chapters or in different parts of one chapter. Dr Anoop Chaturvedi, a teacher of Statistics of Allahabad University, has made, for this study, chi-square tests through a computer both on the basis of total occurrences of *vā* and *ca* in different chapters of a Book (Table 2—some with more *vā-s* and others with more *ca-s*), and in different parts of a few chapters of a similar nature (Table 4) as also of such differences on the basis of occurrences (as in Table 3 and 5).[16a] He is also of the view that chi-square calculations of the total number of *vā-s* and *ca*-s only should be made. Whereas, in the calculations of chi-square, in the former cases (total use of *vā* and *ca*), have proved significant differences in all cases, the tests on the basis of occurrences have not always proved such significant differences.

(c) 20-word block calculations falsifies the results

Even the study of occurrences per sentence is given up in favour of occurrences per 20-word block. The first reason that Trautmann gives for doing so is that[17] 'there is a small and positive correlation between occurrence of particle and length of sentence', though the so-called 'sentences' of equal length are artificial, and tend to falsify the actual calculation of the use of *ca* and *vā* per *real* sentence, for no writer uses *ca* and *vā* on a 20-word block basis in which ordinarily a 20-word block, according to Trautmann's calculation, is more than a sentence or such block may have parts or whole of two or even three sentences.

The result is that in a 20-word block calculation as compared to sentence-wise calculation of occurrences, the chi-square for the former is more significant in a few cases and less significant or equally significant in more cases. For example, in Tables 5 and 6 below are given the chi-square results of occurrences of *vā* and *ca* in seven chapters.[18] Table 5 gives the results of sentence-wise occurrences, and Table 6 those of 20-word block occurrences. On comparison it is found that in no case the chi-square result shows greater significance in the 20-word calculation, in nine cases (for *vā* in Book 5, chapter 2 i.e. one case; and both for *vā* and *ca* in Book 5, chapter 6; Book 6, chapter 2; Book 10, chapter 3; and Book 13, chapter 5, i.e. eight cases) chi-square results show greater significance in sentence-wise calculations and in five cases there is equal significance for both types of calculations.

The real reason for Trautmann's resorting to 20-word block seems to be, however, different. It is that in Gaṅgeśa's *Tattvacintāmaṇi* in which samples from three Books have been considered, if the study of *ca* is made on the basis of occurrences per sentence, Book 1 gives a different result by chi-square testing as compared to the calculation of the other two Books, i.e. Books 2 and 4[19], which means that then Trautmann will have to accept that Gaṅgeśa's *Tattvacintāmaṇi* is a work of two different authors, but Trautmann is not prepared to admit that. It is here that he states another reason for having 20-word block calculations. Trautmann blames the use of *daṇḍa* for this difference in chi-square calculations of the two parts of that work. According to him, '*daṇḍa* was the only mark of punctuation in Sanskrit works and so was used for a variety of purposes other than for ending sentences', and *daṇḍas* are placed differently by different authors. The modern editor's use of *daṇḍa* may be different from the manuscript writer's, and two editors may also use it differently, and sometimes even one editor uses it differently in different parts of a work.[20]

As an example he refers to the Jolly-Schmidt (Lahore) edition and Kangle's edition of the *Arthaśāstra*. Kangle's edition has 22% less *daṇḍas* than in the other edition, the former having 5370 *sūtras* (including verses) as compared to 6880 in the latter. However, this should not have been any reason for Trautmann's turning to the artificial 20-word block basis study. It could have been ascertained by him where a sentence actually ends. A few examples of the two editions are given below. At the end of the second chapter of Book 6 (*Adhikaraṇa* i.e. VI–2) Jolly–Schmidt has written:

Yadi vā paśyet. Amitro me śaktiyukto vākdaṇḍapāruṣyārthaduṣaṇaiḥ prakṛtīrupahaniṣyati. Siddhiyukto vā mṛgayādyūtamadyastrībhiḥ pramādaṃ gamiṣyati. Sa viraktprakṛtirupakṣīṇaḥ pramatto vā sādhyo me bhaviṣyati. Vigrahāyukto vā sarvāsandohanaikastho. Durgastho vā sthāsyati. Sa sahitasainyo mitradurgaviyuktaḥ sādhyo me bhaviṣyati. Balavānvā rājā parataḥ śatrumucchettukāmastamucchidyamānamucchindyāditi balavatā prārthitasya me vipanna karmārambhasya vā sāhāyyaṃ dāsyati. Madhyamalipsāyāṃ ceti. Evamādiṣu kāraṇeṣvamitrasyāpi śaktiṃ siddhiṃ cecchati.

These ten sentences of Jolly–Schmidt's edition are placed as one sentence in Kangle's edition with some verbal differences. The translation of this passage from Kangle's edition (Part II: 6.2.38) is quoted below to facilitate one to understand what a sentence can mean. "Or, if he were to see, 'My enemy, possessed of power, will injure his subjects with verbal or physical injury or appropriation of their property, or, when endowed with success, will become negligent because of (addiction to) hunting, gambling, wine or women, thus with subjects disaffected or (himself) become weakened or remiss, he will be easy to overpower for me; or being attacked in war, he will remain in one place or not in his fort, with all his troops collected together, thus with his army brought together, (and himself) separated from his ally and fort, he will be easy to overpower for me; or he will render help to me when I am attacked by a strong king, (thinking) "the strong king is desirous of exterminating my enemy elsewhere; after exterminating him, he might exterminate me" or (help me) when my undertakings have failed, and when seeking to seize the middle king (the enemy's help is needed)'—for these and other reasons he may wish power and success even to the enemy." Now, 'Or, if he were to see', cannot be a sentence in any case as it is in Jolly–Schmidt's edition. Secondly, the last portion, i.e. 'for these and other reasons, he may wish power and success to the enemy', is a qualifying phrase which applies to all the previous portions of this passage. Therefore, the above passage should be taken as one sentence even though, as Trautmann says, the *daṇḍas* in Jolly–Schmidt's edition are fixed by usage.[21] This usage ought to have been rejected when making a sentence-length or sentence-wise study. The same is the case with the *sūtra* 7.1.32 (Kangle) in which 15 *sūtras* of Jolly–Schmidt's edition are found as one *sūtra* in Kangle's edition, where the *sūtra* is 'Remaining at peace. . . he should secure advancement through peace'. Trautmann himself calls this passage 'a single *sūtrā*' or a single sentence where he says long sentences with many *vā-s* are the main reasons for the difference in the use of *vā* in two samples of Book 7.[21a] These are examples of large differences in the *sūtras* of the two editions, but there are smaller examples also. In Book 3, chapter 12, 52 *sūtras* of Kangle's edition are found as 60 *sūtras* in Jolly–Schmidt's. As an example, the 3rd and 4th *sūtras* of Kangle's edition are found as four (3 to 6)*sūtras* of the other edition. The translation of these two *sūtras* of Kangle's edition is given below for understanding the position and the numbers of *sūtras* of Jolly–Schmidt's edition are given in brackets: '3(3)—The user of the deposit shall pay charges for use in accordance with the place and time, (4) and a fine of twelve *paṇas*. 4(5)—He shall be liable for what is lost or has perished in consequence of the use and (shall pay) a fine of twenty-four *paṇas*, (6) or, if the (deposit) runs away for some other reason.' Here also one can understand whether sentences are to be taken as those found in Kangle's edition or as those in the Jolly–Schmidt edition.

Not only this. Just as Trautmann thinks that a *sūtra* has been placed differently by different copyists or editors and has no fixed connotation, similarly the question may arise what does the word 'word' mean when calculating the 20-word block. Is a compound word, formed by joining two or more words by *sandhis* and *samāsas*, to be taken as one word? Trautmann does not accept this, as in that case the various indeclinables, including *vā* and *ca*, cannot be always separately counted. Therefore, what Trautmann has done is, as can be seen from his calculations of 20-word blocks in Books 6 and 11,[22] that he has taken each compound as one word whether that compound consists of two words or eight. It seems he has not followed the right method. Each word of a compound should have been counted separately as has been indicated by him on p. 100 with *Nītivākyāmṛta's* 24.14 *sūtra* as an example.

In spite of these objections Trautmann's method has been accepted for the purpose of examining his thesis, i.e. the calculation of *vā* and *ca* has been done for differentiating various portions which come from different statistical populations. Secondly, not only has the total use of *ca* and *vā* in different Books or chapters or parts of a chapter been taken note of for chi-square testing, but also their occurrence per sentence. Thirdly, the study of occurrences per 20-word block has been adopted, in addition to the counting of occurrences on the sentence basis, wherever it was possible, i.e. only while studying the differing use of *vā* and *ca* in different portions of some chapters. In other calculations the 20-word block system could not be adopted without the facility or ability to use the computer, and Trautmann himself accepts that the counting of occurrences per 20-word block would have been for him impracticable unaided by computer.[23] In any case as indicated above[24] it has been found that there is, at most places, not much, though of course some, difference, but at some places very great difference in the chi-square testing of portions coming from different statistical populations when *vā*-s and *ca*-s are counted on a sentence basis and on a 20-word block basis.

2. Examination of Statistical Conclusions of Trautmann

While drawing statistical conclusions a preliminary assumption of Trautmann is:[25] 'We will wish to treat the Books as if they were independent treatises in the first instance'. Even though he finds that there is a significant difference for *vā* in the two halves of Book 7[26], one of the two words of high frequency, yet he finally draws his conclusions of treating each Book as a whole (even Book 7, on the ground that 'once it is agreed that here we have to do with a single author, the true distribution ought to fall between the two extremes'). Trautmann nowhere gives any reasons for his doing so (treating each separate Book as a whole), and it appears that probably he did so not for any scientific reason, but probably because it made his task of drawing his statistical conclusions easier, on the ground of the use of *ca* and *vā*. Trautmann emphasizes that *ca* has been used more in Book 2 and less in Books 7 and 9; while in the case of *vā* it is quite the contrary. On the ground of the chi-square tests for these Books, Trautmann concludes that Book 2, on the one hand, and Books 7 and 9, on the other hand, do not come from 'a single population'.[27]

(a) Different chapters of various Books not coming from the same population

It may for once be accepted that Trautmann's conclusion is correct and that Book 2, as contrasted with Books 7 and 9, is different because of the different use of *ca* and *vā*, and that the former and the latter do not come from a single population. If this conclusion is accepted, another conclusion will also have to be accepted, namely, that not only the Books but some chapters from these Books, in comparison to other chapters of the same Books, do not come from a single population. For example, in Book 5 in three chapters (1, 2 and 6), there are markedly more *vā-s* and in three others (3, 4, 5) there are markedly more *ca-s*. The figures are: in 5.1, 49 *vā-s* and 3 *ca-s*, in 5.2, 39 *vā-s* and 21 *ca-s*, and in 5.6, 24 *vā-s* and 17 *ca-s*. On the other hand, in 5.3, 6 *vā-s* and 21 *ca-s*, in 5.4, 2 *vā-s* and 12 *ca-s*, in 5.5, 3 *vā-s* and 9 *ca-s*. The total comes to 112 *vā-s* and 41 *ca*-s for chapters 1, 2 and 6 with 168 *sūtras* (nearly 3:1), as compared to 11 *vā-s* and 42 *ca*-s with 70 *sūtras* (nearly 1:4) for the other chapters. In Book 6 with 2 chapters only, while chapter 1 with 14 *sūtras* has 1 *vā* and 5 *ca-s*, chapter 2 with 38 *sūtras* has 14 *vā-s* and 7 *ca-s*, though in the case of *vā* in the 2nd chapter, as only one sentence has 7 occurrences of *vā*,[28] the results of chi-square calculations on the basis of total number of *vā-s* and *ca*-s and, on the basis of their sentence-wise occurrences, are likely to be different. It would be better, however, to speak of Books 2, 3, 7 and 9 as Trautmann's whole thesis is based on these Books (though he has given chi-square figures for other Books also, but only with reference to Books 2, 3, and 7). In Book 9, whereas chapters 2 to 7 have 135 *vā-s* and 58 *ca-s*, (proportionately 2 times more *vā-s*), chapter 1, which compares 3 kinds of powers (*mantraśakti*, *prabhuśakti*, and *utsāhaśakti*) and deals with the place and time useful for and the power necessary for marching, has only 6 *vā-s* and 25 *ca*-s (proportionately 4 times more *cas*). In Book 7 the middle chapters dealing with pacts for purposes of allies, money, land and undertakings (chapters 9 and 12 as also chapter 13—see pp. 89, 92 below) have less *vā-s* and more *ca*-s (36 and 56), though the other chapters have far more *vā-s* as compared to *ca*-s (278 and 91). In Book 3 whose subject is sixteen titles of law while chapters 2 to 16 dealing with civil law have 180 *vā-s* and 135 *ca*-s (though the difference is not as great as in Books 7 and 11) in the last four chapters, dealing with criminal law, together with the first chapter having procedural law as its subjects, there are markedly less *vā-s* and more *ca*-s (21 and 46). In Book 2 whose subject-matter is state administration, while on the whole there are less *vā-s* and more *ca-s*[29] in two of the chapters there are more *vā-s* and less *ca-s*, i.e. in chapters 3 (21 *vā-s* and 8 *ca-s*) and 14 (26 *vā-s* and 14 *ca-s*). The chi-square test results of all these above-mentioned differences, both based on the difference in the total number of *vā-s* and *ca*-s and based on occurrences per sentence are stated hereafter (Table 2 and Table 3 below). The conclusion, according to Trautmann's main argument, would be that the various chapters (mentioned above) of the aforesaid Books and the other chapters of those Books do not come from the same population, and, therefore, these sets of chapters have not been authored by the same persons.

(b) Different portions of some chapters also do not come from the same population

It can also be noted that not only different chapters of a Book come from different populations, but even different portions of some chapters also come from different populations. For example, in 1.13 the first 14 *sūtras* (sentences—about five 20-word blocks... in Kangle's edition), where there is a discussion of the origin of state, have six *ca*-s and zero or no *vā-s*, whereas the later part of the chapter, i.e. eleven *sūtras* (a little more than five 20-word blocks) have 7 *vā-s* and 3 *ca-s*. In another chapter of the same Book (1.18) the first seven *sūtras* (three 20-word blocks) have 2 *vā-s* and 5 *ca*-s though the next eight *sūtras* (also with three 20-word blocks) which advise the prince as to how to stir up revolt against and kill the king, who, in spite of the best and rightful efforts of the prince, treats him unfairly, there are 7 *vā-s* and 1 *ca*. Similarly, in 5.2, *sūtras* 1–30 (more than eight 20-word blocks) where emergency taxation has been mentioned, there are 6 *vā-s* as compared to 10 *ca-s*. On the other hand, in the next 39 *sūtras* (nearly seventeen 20-word blocks) which advise dubious methods of raising money, there are 33 *vā-s* and only 11 *ca-s*. In this very Book, in the 6th chapter Kauṭilya asks the minister (*Amātya*—here it seems to refer to the chief minister) to see to it that sovereignty of the kingdom is retained in the deceased king's family. In *sūtras* 8 to 30 (nearly eight 20-word blocks) cunning methods for this purpose have been recommended by Kauṭilya and against this purpose by Bhāradvāja. This part had 17 *vā-s* and 3 *ca-s*. In the other *sūtras* (20 in all, nine 20-word blocks), where righteous methods for this purpose are found, there are 7 *vā-s* and 15 *ca-s*. Again, in the last four *sūtras* of 6.2 (five 20-word blocks), there are 10 *vā-s* and 3 *ca-s*, while in the previous 34 *sūtras* (ten 20-word blocks) which describe the *maṇḍala* theory, the number of *ca*-s and *vā-s* is equal (4 and 4). In 10.3 there is a difference between the first 25 *sūtras* (nearly eight 20-word blocks, where one finds the way in which the army is to be made to fight the enemy, including trickery) with 14 *vā-s* and 1 *ca* and *sūtras* 26–56 (excluding verses; ten 20-word blocks), where an army's preparation for war is found with 4 *vā-s* and 14 *ca-s*. In another chapter (13.5), in which ways of pacifying a conquered territory have been detailed, two kinds of methods have been mentioned—righteous (1–14 and 22–23, and six 20-word blocks) and political (15–21, three 20-word blocks), the former having 1 *vā* and 20 *ca*-s and the latter 6 *vā-s* and 4 *ca-s*. An objection may be raised about the figures given above, that they are not within testable limits. Even if that is so, there is no other way to point out the differences in the use of *ca* and *vā* in different parts of a chapter or in different chapters of a Book except by giving these figures and by testing them in whatever manner it may be possible. Therefore, on the basis of the above figures and their chi-square tests given below, if this difference in 'population', (whether between different Books of the *Arthaśāstra*, or between different chapters of a Book, or between different portions of a chapter of that work) is due to different authorship, then the problem, as to which portion has been written by which author, becomes very complicated.

(c) The crucial question of context

The question that now arises is, what is the basis of this difference in population in all the above-mentioned groups. After saying that *ca* has been used more in Book 2 and less in Books 7 and 9, while in case of *vā* it is quite the contrary, and then stating that it may be because of difference in authorship, Trautmann accepts that[30] 'this assumption cannot pass untested, for there are other possible sources of significant divergence, of which the most serious is context'. In spite of it, without examining the context in the use of *ca* and *vā* in different Books of the *Arthaśāstra*, he proceeds to verify his conclusions from texts of known authorship covering a variety of subjects which he calls the 'Control Material'. Even after that he does not try to understand the difference of context in the *Arthaśāstra* itself, spoken of above, but says that[31] 'the divergences noted[32] are not due to subject-matter has been demonstrated'. It may be that it has been demonstrated in the study of the 'Control Material' that he used, but one fails to understand how he has demonstrated it in relation to the different Books of the *Arthaśāstra*.

Here the relation of subject-matter with the use of *ca* and *vā* may be discussed. In the later Books (7 and 9) there has been a necessity to discuss various alternatives regarding the use of six measures of foreign policy and the various ways of conducting war. An example is being given here (7.2. Trautmann has given another example from 7.1)[33] '*Or*, if situated between two stranger kings, he should seek shelter with one capable of protecting him, *or* with one whose intervening neighbour he may be, *or* with both. . . *Or*, he should employ dissention between the two by falsely implicating one against the other and (use) "silent punishment" when they are in discord. *Or*, if situated at the side of two strong kings, he should take steps against immediate danger. *Or*, taking shelter in a fort, he should resort to the dual policy. *Or*, he should act on motives for resorting to peace *or* war. (13, 15–19).' Other examples from Books 7 and 9 can be cited, but what should be clear from the above is that here only *vā* (*or*) could have been used and not *ca* and whosoever be the author he would have to do it, and that the greater use of *vā* here cannot determine authorship.

The greater use of *ca* and *vā* is therefore due to context. This is apparent from Book 2, in which, according to Trautmann more *ca*-s have been used. In the first sample of this Book, whose figures are given at p. 83[34] of *Kauṭilya and the Arthaśāstra*, the total numbèr of *vā*-s used are 54 in ten chapters, out of which 21 are used in one chapter (3) only. Therefore, the writer of this Book is not chary of using *vā*, only that he does not feel the necessity of using *vā* at other places.

At this point it is convenient to consider the contexts of the difference in the use of *ca* and *vā* in different parts of the *Arthaśāstra*. One finds that ordinarily, where the writer discussed the use of political methods or politics, whether internal politics (chapter 5.1) or interstate politics, there has been a greater use of *vā*, while at other places which may be termed theoretical, or at least less political, i.e. where non-political moves have been mentioned, more *ca*-*s* have been used. This would be apparent from a perusal of those chapters, where in one part of the chapter there is more frequent use of *ca* and, in another part more of *vā*. For example, in 1.13, where the writer puts forward his theory of the origin of state, only *ca* is found and there is no *vā*[35], while in the later portion[36], where the writer advises the king about how to deal with different kinds of persons within the state by using the four *upāyas*, he feels the necessity of using more *vā*-*s* than *ca*-s (7 *vā*-*s* and 3 *ca*-*s*). In 6.2 practically the whole of the chapter is occupied with the *maṇḍala* theory of interstate relations in which there are equal number of *ca*-s and *vā*-*s*, but in the last four *sūtras*, where the writer deals with interstate politics, the use of *vā* substantially increases (10 *vā*-*s* and 3 *ca*-*s*). In the 18th chapter of the first Book, which deals with the relation between the prince and the king, in the first seven *sūtras* where the prince is asked to obey the king etc., there are 2 *vā*-*s* and 7 *ca*-s but in the next eight *sūtras*, in which the prince is asked somehow to gather strength and kill an incorrigible king, there are 7 *vā*-*s* and only one *ca*. The position of 5.2; 5.6; 10.3 and 13.5 has been already stated (pp. 85–6 above) and nothing needs to be added here. The other context, where more *vā*-*s* have been used, is about the construction of a palace or of a fort.[37]

For the same reasons, it seems, there is a greater use of *vā* in some chapters of a Book and less in others. This is most explicit in Book 5 in which chapters 3 (salaries of government servants), 4 (conduct proper for a dependent) and 5 (proper behaviour of a courtier), which are comparatively more theoretical, have more *ca*-s (42 *ca*-s and 11 *vā-s*), while chapters 1, 2 and 6 (more political) have more *vā-s* (41 *ca*-s and 112 *vā-s*). There are internal differences also in chapters 2 and 6, but they have been noted earlier. Likewise Book 6, chapter 1, prescribes the qualities of constituent elements of a state, has 1 *vā* and 5 *ca-s*, whereas chapter 2, more political in nature, has 14 *vā-s* and 7 *ca*-s (here again the internal difference in 6.2 has been examined before). Again, in Book 7, the section, which deals with treaties for securing an ally, money, land and undertaking in four chapters (9 to 12 as also 13), has more *ca*-s and less *vā-s* (36 *vā-s* and 56 *ca-s*) compared to other chapters (278 *vā-s* and 91 *ca-s)*. In these chapters the author compares the comparative usefulness of these treaties and of the gains arising from them. This kind of comparative discussion (i.e. less political) continues in the 13th chapter also, but not in connection with treaties. These five chapters which seem to be more theoretical (like Book 8) have 36 *vā-s* and 56 *ca-s*, chapter 9 being an exception. Chapter 1 of Book 9 dealing with relative strength of the three Powers (*śaktis*), place and time of war and seasons for marching on an expedition (sections 135 and 136), a comparatively theoretical subject as compared to actual tactics of fighting, has 25 *ca*-s and 6 *vā-s*, whereas the other chapters have altogether 58 *ca*-s and 135 *vā-s*. In Book 10, which has on the whole more *ca*-s than *vā-s* (61:51), chapters 2, 3, 5 and 6, which deal with methods of fighting against the enemy (*Kūṭayuddha* and *Prakāśayuddha)*, have 48 *vā-s* and 35 *ca*-s as against chapters 1 (setting up of the camp) and 4 (section 153 which discusses grounds suitable for fighting and section 154 which discusses functions of the infantry and cavalry, the chariots and the elephants) have 3 *vā-s* and 26 *ca-s*. In Book 13, chapter 5, which is, on the whole, more theoretical and deals with pacification of a conquered territory has 7 *vā-s* and 24 *ca-s*, while chapters 1 to 4 have 110 *vā-s* and 53 *ca-s*. In Book 2, chapter 3, which deals with the construction of fort (chapter 1, 20.1–13 dealing with construction of a palace and has 7 *vā-s* and 4 *ca-s*), has 21 *vā-s* and 8 *ca-s*, while the other 35 chapters have 225 *vā-s* and 481 *ca-s*. In Book 3, the last four chapters dealing with criminal law together with chapter 1 (legal procedure) have 21 *vā-s* and 46 *ca-s*, whereas, the other chapters which have civil law as their subject have 180 *vā-s* and 135 *ca-s*. In this case, it is difficult to state the exact reasons behind this difference, but this difference clearly seems to be based on the subject-matter.

It is true that the number of chapters mentioned above, which are against the general trend, in the use of *ca* and *vā* because of the difference in subject-matter, is not very large (only 19 chapters) but they are sufficient to prove that some chapters of a Book do not come from the same population as do the others of the same Book. When, however, taken with the total number of other chapters (one hundred andtwenty) which contain theoretical, or non-political discussions and have more *ca-s* than *vā-s*, and those which contain discussions of political or fighting methods and have more *vā-s* than *ca-s*, then the number of such chapters together does not remain small, but add up to nearly one hundred and forty. This also shows that the difference in the use of *ca* and *vā* is based on subject-matter and not on authorship. There are, of course, some exceptions where the subject being non-political, use of more *ca-s* would be expected, or where the subject being political, use of more *vā-s* would be expected—but it is not so in fact. However, throughout the whole treatise the number of such chapters seems to be only 10 out of 148 chapters. These chapters are 2.14; 4.1, 8 and 12; 7.9 and 16; 8.2; 12.2 and 3 and 13.1.[38]

This also shows that Trautmann's primary assumption that each Book has to be treated as a whole is wrong, at least about 8 Books i.e. Books 2, 3, 5, 6, 7, 9, 10, 13. Book 11 has only one chapter. Only three Books (4, 8 and 12) have to be taken as a whole, in spite of the differing use of *ca* and *vā* in different chapters. Books 1 and 14 are throughout similar in subject-matter and throughout these Books there is ordinarily a greater use of *ca* (Book 1) or a greater use of *vā* (Book 14).

Just as in different portions of some chapters, as also in different chapters of some Books, those portions or those chapters where the discussions are of more theoretical and less political in nature, there is a greater use of *ca*, whereas such chapters or portions of chapters, which deal with political or military tactics, there is a greater use of *vā*, similarly Books 1, 2, 8 which contain more theoretical discussion have more *ca-s*.[39] On the other hand, those Books, which deal with political (both internal and external) and military tactics have more *vā-s*. These are Books 5 (on the whole), 7, 9, 11, 12, and 13.[40] Books 3 and 4 nearly come in the middle category.[41] Book 6 with 15 *vā-s* and 12 *ca*-s and Book 10 with 61 *ca*-s and 51 *vā-s* can also be placed in this category. Therefore, it seems that the difference between different Books (as a whole), or between different chapters of a Book are for contextual reasons, and Trautmann's thesis that these differences are due to difference in authorship does not seem to be correct.

The tables below give chi-square test results of the differences in the use of *ca* and *vā* in different chapters of a Book, and of such difference between different portions of a chapter. For all these tests I am very grateful to Dr G.S. Pandey and Dr Anoop Chaturvedi, both of the Statistics Department of Allahabad University. Dr Pandey gave me the chi-square table, explaining to me the method of calculating chi-square and mean and variance. Dr Chaturvedi has made the chi-square calculations for me on the computer and they are of two types. On one table, the chi-square results have been given on the basis of differences in the total number of *ca*-s and *vā*-s used in the two parts of a Book or of a chapter and in the next table such chi-square results are given on the basis of difference in occurrences of *ca* and *vā* per sentence therein.

TABLE II

Calculation of chi-square on the basis of total number of *ca*-s and *vā*-*s* used in two parts of a Book:

Book 2 - chapter 3 and the rest

Chapter 3 — 33 sentences or (*sūtras*)	Rest — 1182 sentences
21 *vā*-*s* and 8 *ca*-*s*	225 *vā*-*s* and 481 *ca*-*s*

x^2 = 20.564, d.f. (degrees of freedom) 1, highly significant result.

Book 3 - chapters 1 and 17–20, and the rest

Chapter 1 and 17–20 — 114 sentences	Rest — 554 sentences
21 *vā*-*s* and 46 *ca*-*s*	180 *vā*-*s* and 135 *ca*-*s*

x^2 = 14.750, d.f. 1, highly significant result.

Book 5 - chapters 3 – 5, and the rest

Chapter 3 – 5 — 70 sentences	Rest — 168 sentences
11 *vā*-*s* and 42 *ca*-*s*	112 *vā*-*s* and 41 *ca*-*s*

x^2 = 45.010, d.f. 1, highly significant result.

Book 7 - chapters 9–13, and the rest 13 chapters

Chapter 9 – 13 — 183 sentences	Rest — 411 sentences
36 *vā*-*s* and 56 *ca*-*s*	278 *vā*-*s* and 91 *ca*-*s*

x^2 = 44.451, d.f. 1, highly significant result.

Book 9 - chapters 1 and 5 other chapters

Chapter 1–51 sentences	Chapters 2–6–281 sentences
6 *vā-s* and 25 *ca-s*	135 *vā-s* and 58 *ca-s*

x^2 = 25.313 d.f. 1, highly significant.

Book 10 - chapters 1 and 4, and other 4 chapters

Chapters 1 and 4 — 33 sentences	Other chapters–176 sentences
3 *vā-s* and 26 *ca-s*	48 *vā-s* and 35 *ca-s*

x^2 = 19.540, d.f. 1, highly significant.

Book 13 - chapter 5 and the rest four chapters

Chapter 5–23 sentences	Chapter1–4—182 sentences
7 *vā-s* and 24 *ca-s*	110 *vā-s* and 53 *ca-s*

x^2 = 21.940, d.f. 1, highly significant.

It will be seen in the above table that in each Book the difference between two groups of chapters is highly significant. Trautmann considers that where the deviation between observed and expected values through sampling variation is less than .1% (i.e. one out of a thousand or more cases), then that should be considered 'highly significant', where it is 1% (one out of 100 or more cases), that is 'significant' and where it is 5% (one out of 20 or more cases), that is 'probably significant'. The same criteria has been adopted here. At one degree (d.f.) according to the table, if the chi-square is 10.83 or more it is 'highly significant', if the chi-square is between 6.63 and 10.83 it is 'significant', and if the chi-square is between 3.84 and 6.63 it is 'probably significant'. At two degrees of freedom if the chi-square is more than 13.81 it is 'highly significant', if the chi-square is between 9.21 and 13.81 it is 'significant' and if chi-square is between 5.99 and 9.21 it is 'probably significant'. 'Significant' means that in sampling variation there is very little chance of the two portions of a Book or of a chapter coming from the same population.

TABLE III

Chi-square result of the above groups of chapters of the above Books on the basis of occurrences of *ca* and *vā* per sentence *(sūtra)*:

Book 2 - chapter 3 (33 sentences) and the rest (1182 sentences)

*Occurrences per sentence of *vā*

Occurrences	Chapter –3	Rest
0	20	993
1	10	159
2+ (two or more occurrences)	3	30

$x^2 = 13.793$, d.f. 2, significant.

*Occurrences per sentence of *ca*

Occurrences	Chapter - 3	Rest
0	25	781
1+	8	401

$x^2 = 1.348$, d.f. 1, insignificant.

Book 3 - chapters 1 and 17–20 (sentences 114), and the rest (554 sentences)

*Occurrences per sentence of *vā*

Occurrences	Chapters 1, 17–20	Rest
0	97	404
1	13	123
2+	4	27

$x^2 = 7.660$, d.f. 2, probably significant.

*Occurrences per sentence of *ca*

Occurrences	Chapters 1, 17–20	Rest
0	78	436
1	31	103
2 +	5	15

$x^2 = 5.674$, d.f. 2, insignificant.

Book 5 - chapters 3–5 (70 sentences) and the rest, chapters 1, 2, and 6 (168 sentences)

*Occurrences per sentence of *vā*

Occurrences	Chapters 3–5	Rest
0	59	92
1	11	55
2+	0	21

x^2 =18.571, d.f. 2, highly significant.

*Occurrences per sentence of *ca*

Occurrences	Chapters 3–5	Rest
0	37	130
1	27	35
2+	6	3

x^2 = 14.197 d.f. 2, highly significant.

Book 7 - chapters 9–13 (183 sentences) and the rest 14 chapters (411 sentences)

*Occurrences per sentences of *vā*

Occurrences	Chapters 9–13	Rest
0	150	251
1	31	108
2+	2	52

x^2 = 31.518 d.f. 2, highly significant.

*Occurrences per sentence of *ca*

Occurrences	Chapters 9–13	Rest
0	139	341
1	34	51
2+	10	19

x^2 = 4.323 d.f. 2, insignificant.

Book 9 - chapter 1 (51 sentences) and other 5 chapters (281 sentences)

*Occurrences per sentence of *vā*

Occurrences	Chapter 1	Rest
0	46	197
1	4	59
2+	1	25

x^2 = 8.205 d.f. 2, probably significant.

*Occurrences per sentence of *ca*

Occurrences	Chapter 1	Rest
0	37	234
1	7	38
2+	7	9

$x^2 = 11.886$, d.f. 2, significant.

Book 10 - chapters 1 and 4 (33 sentences), and the rest 4 chapters (176 sentences)

*Occurrences per sentence of *vā*

Occurrences	Chapters 1 and 4	Rest
0	31	137
1+	2	39

$x^2 = 4.567$, d.f. 1, probably significant.

* Occurrences per sentences of *ca*

Occurrences	Chapter 1, 4	Rest
0	13	145
1+	20	31

$x^2 = 27.844$, d.f. 1, highly significant.

Book 13 - chapter 5 (23 sentences) and the other four chapters (182 sentences)

*Occurrences per sentence of *vā*

Occurrences	Chapter 5	Rest
0	18	96
1+	5	86

$x^2 = 5.385$, d.f. 1, probably significant.

*Occurrences per sentence of *ca*

Occurrences	Chapter 5	Rest
0	6	139
1	12	33
2+	5	10

$x^2 = 26.456$, d.f. 2, highly significant.

It will be seen in the above table that only in Books 2, 3 and 7, and that too only in the case of *ca*, is the chi-square result insignificant, otherwise the results are, to a greater or lesser extent, significant, so, the two groups of chapters do not come from the same population.

In the following two tables chi-square test results of some chapters are given, in which, in one portion of the chapter, there has been a greater use of *vā*, and in the other portion, that of *ca*. In Table 4, chi-square test results on the basis of the total number of *vā-s* and *ca*-s used in two portions are to be found and in Table 5 are to be found such results on the basis of occurrences of *vā* and *ca* in the two portions.

TABLE IV

Book 1 - chapter 13 (*sūtras* 1–14 and *sūtras* 15–25)

Sentences 1–14	Sentences 15–25
0 *vā-s* and 6 *ca-s*	7 *vā-s* and 3 *ca-s*

x^2 = 7.467, d.f. 1, significant.

Book 1 - chapter 18 (sentences 1–7 and sentences 8–15)

Sentences 1–7	Sentences 8–15
2 *vā-s* and 5 *ca-s*	7 *vā-s*, 1 *ca*

x^2 = 5.402, d.f. 1, probably significant.

Book 5 - chapter 2 (sentences 1–30 and sentences 31–69)

Sentences 1–30	Sentences 31–69
6 *vā-s* and 10 *ca-s*	33 *vā-s* and 11 *ca-s*

x^2 = 7.253, d.f. 1, significant.

Book 5 - chapter 6 (sentences 8–30 and the rest 20 sentences)

Sentences 8–30	Rest
17 *vā-s* and 3 *ca-s*	7 *vā-s*, 15 *ca-s*

x^2 = 12.099, d.f. 1, highly significant.

Book 6 - chapter 2 (sentences 1–34 and sentences 35–38)

Sentences 1–34	Sentences 35–38
4 *vā-s* and 4 *ca-s*	10 *vā-s* and 3 *ca-s*

x^2 = 1.615, d.f. 1, insignificant.

Book 10 - chapter 3 (sentences 1–25 and sentences 26–56).
(Two verses in the middle are left out.)

Sentences 1–25	Sentences 26–56
14 *vā-s* and 1 *ca*	4 *vā-s* and 14 *ca-s*

x^2 = 16.687, d.f. 1, highly significant.

Book 13 - chapter 5 (sentences 15–21 and other 16 sentences)

Sentences 15–21	Sentences 1–14, 22–23
6 *vā-s* and 4 *ca-s*	1 *vā* and 20 *ca-s*

x^2 = 11.824, d.f. 1, highly significant.

In the above table the chi-square result of only 6 is insignificant, otherwise all results are significant.

TABLE V

Book 1 - chapter 13; sentences 1–14, and sentences 15–25

*Occurrences of *vā* per sentences

Occurrences	1–14	15–25
0	14	6
1+	0	5

x^2 = 7.955 d.f. 1, significant.

*Occurrences of *ca* per sentence

Occurrence	1–14	15–25
0	9	8
1+	5	3

x^2 = .014 d.f. 1, insignificant.

Book 1 - chapter 18; sentences 1–7, and sentences 8–15

*Occurrences per sentence of *vā*

Occurrences	1 to 7	8 to 15
0	5	2
1+	2	6

x^2 = 3.2333. d.f. 1, insignificant.

*Occurrences per sentence of *ca*

Occurrences	1–7	8–15
0	3	7
1+	4	1

x^2 = 3.348 d.f. 1, insignificant.

Book 5 - chapter 2; sentences 1–30, and sentences 31–69

*Occurrences per sentence of *vā*

Occurrences	1–30	31–69
0	26	15
1+	4	24

x^2 = 16.341, d.f. 1, highly significant.

*Occurrences per sentence of *ca*

Occurrences	1–30	31–69
0	20	30
1+	10	9

x^2 = .894, d.f. 1, insignificant.

Book 5 - chapter 6; sentences 8–30, and the rest

*Occurrences per sentences of *vā*

Occurrences	8–30 (23)	Rest (20)
0	8	14
1+	15	6

x^2 =5.310, d.f. 1, probably significant.

*Occurrences per sentences of *ca*

Occurrences	8–30 (23)	Rest (20)
0	20	6
1+	3	14

x^2 =15.213, d.f. 1, highly significant.

Book 6 - chapter 2; sentences 1–34, and sentences 35–38

*Occurrences per sentence of *vā*

Occurrences	1–34	35–38
0	31	1
1+	3	3

x^2 =11.788, d.f. 1, highly significant.

*Occurrences per sentence of *ca*

Occurrences	1–34	35–38
0	30	2
1+	4	2

x^2 =3.935, d.f. 1, probably significant.

Book 10 - chapter 3, sentences 1–25 and sentences 26 to 56

* Occurrences per sentence of *vā*

Occurrences	1–25	26–56
0	12	25
1+	13	4

x^2 =9.086, d.f. 1, significant.

*Occurrences per sentence of *ca*

Occurrences	1–25	26–56
0	24	17
1+	1	12

x^2 =10.263, d.f. 1, significant.

Book 13 - chapter 5; sentences 15–21, and other sentences 1–14 and 22–23

*Occurrences per sentence of *vā*

Occurrences	15–21	Rest
0	3	15
1+	4	1

x^2 = 7.413, d.f. 1, significant.

*Occurrences per sentence of *ca*

Occurrences	15–25	Rest
0	4	2
1+	3	14

x^2 =5.033, d.f. 1, probably significant.

Here also only in two chapters and that too in the case of *ca* only and in one chapter for both *ca* and *vā* is the result insignificant. Otherwise the two groups of sentences do not come from the same population.

TABLE VI

This table gives the chi-square test results of the 0 and 1+ occurrences of *vā* and *ca* per 20-word block for those chapters of the *Arthaśāstra* where in one part of the chapter there are greater occurrences of *vā* and in the other part there are greater occurrences of *ca*. This table when compared with Table V will show the difference between chi-square results of occurrences per sentence and of occurrences per 20-word block. Thus it also demonstrates the reason of Trautmann's resorting to chi-square testing per 20-word block of Gaṅgeśa's *Tattvacintāmaṇi* instead of the testing on the basis of occurrences per sentence of the work. The reason is that ordinarily the chi-square test results become insignificant in the former case and eliminates the difference between Book 1 and Books 2 and 4 of that work. It will be seen that the significance of difference is lessened, but not totally eliminated.

Book 1 - chapter 13; five 20-word blocks (*sūtras* 1 to 14), and four 20-word blocks (*sūtras* 15 to 25)

*Occurrences of *vā*

Occurrences	5 blocks	4 blocks
0	5	0
1+	0	4

x^2 =9.000 d.f. 1, significant.

Occurrences of *ca*

Occurrences	5 blocks	4 blocks
0	1	2
1+	4	2

x^2 = .900, d.f. 1, insignificant.

Book 1 - chapter 18; three 20-word blocks (*sūtras* 1 to 7), and three 20-word blocks (*sūtras* 8 to 13)

*Occurrences of *vā*

Occurrences	3 blocks	3 blocks
0	2	0
1+	1	3

x^2 =3.00, d.f. 1, insignificant.

*Occurrences of *ca*

Occurrences	3 blocks	3 blocks
0	0	2
1+	3	1

x^2 = 3.000, d.f. 1, insignificant.

Book 5 - chapter 2; eight 20-word blocks (*sūtras* 1 to 30), and seventeen 20-word blocks (*sūtras* 31–69)

*Occurrences of *vā*

Occurrences	8 blocks	17 blocks
0	4	2
1+	4	15

x^2 = 4.360, d.f. 1, probably significant.

*Occurrences of *ca*

Occurrences	8 blocks	17 blocks
0	2	10
1+	6	7

x^2 =2.493, d.f. 1, insignificant.

Book 5 - chapter 6; eight 20-word block (*sūtras* 8–30), and nine 20-word blocks (Rest of the *sūtras* 1 to 7, 32 to 44).

*Occurrences of *vā*

Occurrences	8 blocks	9 blocks
0	1	3
1+	7	6

x^2 = 1.022, d.f. 1, insignificant.

*Occurrences of *ca*

Occurrences	8 blocks	9 blocks
0	6	3
1+	2	6

x^2 = 2.951, d.f. 1, insignificant.

Book 6 - chapter 2; ten 20-word blocks (*sūtras* 1 to 34), and five 20-word-blocks (*sūtras* 35 to 38)

*Occurrences of *vā*

Occurrences	10 blocks	5 blocks
0	7	1
1+	3	4

x^2 = 3.348, d.f. 1, insignificant.

*Occurrences of *ca*

Occurrences	10 blocks	5 blocks
0	6	2
1+	4	3

x^2 = .536,d.f. 1, insignificant.

Book 10 - chapter 3; eight 20-word blocks (*sūtras* 1 to 26), and ten 20-word blocks (*sūtras* 27 to 29, 33 to 56)

*Occurrences of *vā*

Occurrences	8 blocks	10 blocks
0	1	7
1+	7	3

x^2 =5.951, d.f. 1, probably significant.

*Occurrences of *ca*

Occurrences	8 blocks	10 blocks
0	7	4
1+	1	6

x^2 = 4.219, d.f. 1, probably significant.

Book 13 - chapter 5; three 20-word block (*sūtras* 15–21), and six 20-word blocks (Rest of the *sūtras* 16 *sūtras* 1 to 14, 22–23)

*Occurrences of *vā*

Occurrences	3 blocks	6 blocks
0	0	5
1+	3	1

x^2 =5.625,d.f. 1, probably significant.

*Occurrences of *ca*

Occurrences	3 blocks	6 blocks
0	1	0
1+	2	6

x^2 =2.250, d.f. 1, insignificant.

3. Other Deficiencies of the Theory

(a) Deviation of Trautmann from his own statistics

In spite of the shortcomings of his theory Trautmann's conclusions could at least have the merit of consistency, if he remained true to his own statistics. His contention is that on the basis of statistical data (about *ca* and *vā*), 'The separate authorship of Books 2, 3, and 7 is well established'.[42] He has attempted to group the other Books around these three Books though he seems to have been forced to speak of a fourth group also.[43] He holds that Books 1 and 2 belong together both on the basis of the statistical results as well as from the fact of *their contiguity and subject-matter*. He also proved statistically[44] that 'we could initially consider Books 1, 2 and 8 as forming the work of a single author',[45] but on the next page he adds 'to add Book 8 to that group would, however, make less sense, since it is neither contiguous nor is it obvious that its subject-matter (vices or calamities of the king and seven constituent elements) fits well with the first two'(training of kings and princes; Heads of Departments). 'Book 5 shows a slightly significant divergence in respect of *vā* when compared with Book 3 and the same for *vā* and *ca*, when compared with Book 7, though it clearly cannot be grouped with Book 2.'[46] Even then he concludes 'Books 3 and 4 (law and crime) clearly, form the core of a second group, to which Book 5 "secret conduct" might logically be added'. He does not, however, explicity state the logic behind it. 'Of the rest, objections to grouping Book 3 with any other appear in every case except Book 10'[47]—to which it is statistically similar.[48] This means that it was preferable to group Book 10 with Book 3 and not with Book 7, because of a slightly significant difference with respect to *vā*.[49] Yet he forsakes his statistics here also. 'The third group, then, whose general subject is interstate relations, would consist of Books 7, 9 and 10.' He feels that Book 6 can be put here because it serves as a preface to Book 7, 'but could also for the same reason be a later composition added by the organizer', though Book 6 statistically agrees with Book 3[50] fully, and not so with either Book 2 or 7. 'Books 12 and 13 form a fourth group of miscellaneous subjects under the heading of interstate relations, to which *one would be inclined* to add Books 11 and 14.'[51] Book 8 is not placed in any group. Thus Trautmann has grouped the Books in the following manner. Group I includes Books 1 and 2, while Books 3, 4 and 5 go to form group II, Group III has Books 6, 7, 9 and 10 and group IV consists of Books 11, 12, 13 and 14. As already said Book 8 is not to be found anywhere. Now, if the statistical calculations of Trautmann[52] are considered on the basis of *ca* and *vā* (his main basis pp. 83–88) the Books will have to be grouped in this order—Books 1, 2 and 8 in the first group, Books 3, 4, 6 and 10 in the second group and Books 7, 9, 11 and 14 in the third group. The remaining (Books 5, 12 and 13) may probably form one or, two or three groups because they show significant result with respect to either *ca* or *vā* or both, when compared with Books 2, 3, or 7. This means that his grouping of Books 5, 6, 8, 10, 11 and 14 does not agree with his statistical results. This discrepancy is due to the fact that Trautmann did the grouping of Books mainly on the basis of contiguity, and, to some extent only, on the basis of subject-matter because the subject-matter of Book 5 is wholly different from the other books of its group, and the subject-matter of Books 6, 10 and 14 also is partially different. Trautmann's grouping is based not so much on his statistical calculations. This grouping of

Books on the basis of contiguity could have been done by any educated person, and the heavy statistical method Trautmann applied was not at all necessary for this purpose. Not only that, he seems to be confused as to whether to specify the Books as those composed by four or three authors. While in 'Testing the *Arthaśāstra*' (pp. 114–22), he speaks of only Books 2, 3 and 7 as basic Books and in the beginning of his grouping of Books he tries to group them around these three only, he soon finds the necessity of adding a fourth group and finally differentiates four groups. Again, while trying to assign the dates to authors of different groups of Books he considers only the periods of three authors (pp. 174–185). In the end he again maintains that the *Arthaśāstra* is 'a composite picture to which three or four different individuals have contributed' (p. 186).

(b) Sentence-length and Compound-length study

There are some other facts which militate against Trautmann's three or four author theory of the *Arthaśāstra*. One of them is his sentence-length and compound-length study of the *Arthaśāstra*. His sentence-length study does not go beyond his Control Material, i.e. Gaṅgeśa's *Tattvacintāmaṇi* and Somadeva's *Nītivākyāmṛta*. Thereafter, finding a large difference between the sentence-length distribution for Book 1 and those for Books 2 and 4 of *Tattvacintāmaṇi* and a considerable divergence 'between sample 2 at the one extreme and sample 5 at the other in every part of the sentence-length distribution of *Nītivākyāmṛta*' he does not proceed either to make a sentence-length study of the *Arthaśāstra*, or if he has made that study, he has not incorporated that result in this chapter. He does so on the excuse, which does not seem to be very strong, that *daṇḍas* are being used erratically by writers or copyists of Sanskrit books.[53] However, as said earlier (in this article, pp. 77–81 above), he could have fixed the sentences according to his own thinking, and, then could have shown whether his sentence-length study of the *Arthaśāstra* confirms or not his earlier grouping of Books of that work on the basis of the use of *ca* and *vā*. He himself says in connection with his sentence-length study that 'if *daṇḍa* were confined to the functions of the period and were intelligently inserted by editors, the sentence-length test would be much easier to apply' and he could have done that.

About the compound-length study of the *Arthaśāstra* his results are found at pp. 130–31 of his book. He emphasizes three facts: (1) That on the basis of that (i.e. compound-length) calculation, Book 2 is different from Books 3 and 7, supporting his conclusion of difference in authorship. (2) That Books 3 and 5 may be considered homogenous (a fact which, because of his statistical calculation regarding these books,[54] does not wholly agree with this conclusion). (3) That the association of Book 3 with Book 7 of the *Arthaśāstra* is supported by the compound-length study (though he had previously stated that the separate authorship of Books 3 and 7 is well established).[55] However, what is more important while comparing his statistical conclusion here with his earlier grouping of Books of the *Arthaśāstra*, is that two of his earlier groups are rejected here—that of Books 1 and 2 on the one hand, and of Books 3 and 4 on the other. Only the Books placed around Book 7 (3rd group) are similarly placed here. What is contrary here to the earlier grouping, is that the difference between Books 3 and the group around Book 7 is eliminated because in the compound-length calculations,[56] both Books 3 and 7 not only agree between themselves, but also with Books 6 and 9 and thus Book 3 of one group is coalesced with the third group. Thus all the three earlier groupings of Books for purposes of authorship seem to be unacceptable here—two groups, i.e. the first and the second, have been divided in the compound-length study and the second group, of this earlier grouping, partly appears to have been combined with the third group, in this study by Trautmann.

(c) Control Material

In Trautmann's sentence-length and compound-length study his conclusions about his control material, i.e. Gaṅgeśa's *Tattvacintāmaṇi* and Somadeva's *Nītivākyāmṛta,* are also important.

After making a *sentence-length study* of Gaṅgeśa's *Tattvacintāmaṇi*[57] and a study of the distribution of *ca* in the three samples of *Tattvacintāmaṇi*[58] by sentences, Trautmann finds that a great difference exists between Book 1 on the one hand and Books 2 and 4 on the other, and that the chi-square test also for these Books gives significant results. In the *calculation of means and variance for sentence-length distribution*, Gaṅgeśa's Books 1 and 2 show a great divergence while the agreement between Books 2 and 4 is good,[59] which again means that Book 1 is different from the other two Books. Even the *compound-length distribution* of the three samples of Gaṅgeśa's chi-square shows a 5% significance. In spite of all these differences of Gaṅgeśa's Book 1 with his Books 2 and 4, Trautmann is unable to reconcile with this fact, and holds that it would be absurd to think that the author of Book 1 of Gaṅgeśa is different from the author of Books 2 and 4.[60] It may be because he has taken *Tattvacintāmaṇi* as his Control Material. Therefore, while he wants to prove the unity of authorship of this work, he does not want to equate it with *Arthaśāstra*, where he is set upon to prove different authorship of its different parts. It may also be kept in mind that Trautmann has taken recourse to a 20-word block study of *Tattvacintāmaṇi* because the sentence-wise calculations for *ca* had given a significant result as between Book 1 on the one hand, and Books 2 and 4 on the other.

In Somadeva's *Nītivākyamṛta* also, in the sentence-length study, he finds that a considerable divergence exists between Sample 2 at one extreme and Sample 5 at the other in every part of the distribution,[61] and that the variance ratio between these has a highly significant value.[62] In the compound-length study also the variance ratio, not only between Samples 2 and 4, but also between 2 and 5 is significant.[63] Yet, here again he says the same thing, i.e. that 'it would be absurd to conclude that Samples 2 and 5 of Somadeva. . . have different authors. . . .'[64]

Trautmann, just as he proves that the *Arthaśāstra* has a number of authors, should have honestly accepted that *Tattvacintāmaṇi* and *Nītivākyāmṛta* also (on the ground of his calculations) have more than one author. Or, on the contrary, if he thinks that in spite of all these differences the latter two works in their complete form were written respectively by Gaṅgeśa and Somadeva only, he should also have accepted that the whole of *Arthaśāstra*, as it stands, was also written by a single author, Kauṭilya.

(d) Cross-references

Trautmann admits that there are numerous cross-references within the *Arthaśāstra* which heighten the sense of its unity (p. 69). These cross-references are both direct, i.e. where in it there is specific mention of another part of the work,[65] and indirect, i.e. where words are used technically in the same sense in different parts of the work.[66] In this article the cross-references within those portions which, according to Trautmann, are authored by a single person will not be considered. Only those cross-references will be taken into account which Trautmann thinks, are found in those portions of the *Arthaśāstra* supposedly written by different authors, then such direct references only are more than 90 in number, and such indirect references about 200. These have been calculated on the basis of footnotes in Kangle's English translation of the *Arthaśāstra*, but the number of such references might be more, for Kangle has not mentioned some such references, e.g., a reference to 5.1 in *Arthaśāstra* 7.2.15 or a reference to Book 14 in 9.6.73, probably because Kangle might have considered it to be unnecessary.

In his last chapter (i.e. 7), Trautmann tries to fix the ages of different portions of the *Arthaśāstra*. He only indicates the date of his first group,[67] which, he says, is AD 150.[68] He seems to think that his second group[69] is the earliest of all the groups, for, according to him, it is older than *Dharma Smṛtis*.[70] The dates of the other Books seem to be, in his opinion, between these two dates because the *maṇḍala* doctrine has been carried further in these Books of the *Arthaśāstra*.[71] This chronology of different Books of the *Arthaśāstra* is indirectly contradicted by Trautmann himself when he says that the number of cross-references increases as the work (*Arthaśāstra*) progresses, which shows, at least to some extent, that this work was written in the order in which it is found at present. But if Trautmann's chronology is accepted, these cross-references, which may be called inter-author cross-references, as Trautmann seems to think, must have been the work of an editor (if there was one), at least in those cases where an earlier author's work (whoever he may be) refers to the portion written by a supposedly later writer. Similarly, for the sake of unity of the work, the assumed editor may also have made some other changes or additions in the Books of these so-called earlier writers who, as Trautmann says, are the *Pūrvācāryas* (ancient teachers) whose works have been brought together by the assumed editor or 'organizer (who) called himself Kauṭilya whether rightly or wrongly'.[72] Trautmann says, 'I believe then, that the various hands we detected in the *Arthaśāstra* belong to the *pūrvācāryas*, the previous teachers whose works, in condensed form perhaps, were bound into a single work by a compiler who divided the work into chapters, added the terminal verses, composed the first and last chapters (and possibly one of the long books), and who may have added other original material but did not rework his sources to the extent that their stylistic features were obscured'.[73] He also says,[74] 'that a certain amount of reworking by the organizer and even original writing to provide linkages between the independent works is probable in this theory'. His view that the organizer took other authors' books 'in a condensed form' appears to be based on two passages quoted by Medhātithi from the *Adhyakṣapracāra* (on Manu 7.61, 81, not found in Kauṭilya). *Adhyakṣapracāra* is also mentioned by *Kāmasūtra*.[75] 'It is conceivable that the forbear of Book 2 was a work entitled *Adhyakṣapracāra* dealing with ministers as well as overseers, and that parts of it have contributed to *Arthaśāstra* Book 1, and parts of it were lost through abridgement.'[76] Thus if an editor has abridged and made some changes and added some original material in the books of the previous writer, taken over by him in the *Arthaśāstra*, the use of *ca* and *vā* in the present version becomes the work of the editor, i.e. Kauṭilya and not that of the original writers and so the conclusions based on the whole calculation of *ca* and *vā* by Trautmann become doubtful. Unless these abridgements and changes can be specifically proved, this calculation cannot specify the so-called original writers of different Books as has been done by Trautmann.

(e) Lacunae of the statistical method exemplified

Trautmann honestly accepts that there are lacunae in the statistical method, particularly with regard to the *Arthaśāstra*. He says that the problem of authorship of a classical work is not very difficult to solve. If the authorship of a text is disputed between two or more authors, other works of those authors are available as Control Material. From these works can be selected: (1) words of high frequency, (2) words which are evenly distributed within authors, and (3) words which have different rates of distribution between authors. In the case of the *Arthaśāstra*, other works of Trautmann's supposedly different writers are not available, not even the *Adhyakṣapracāra*, which he mentions twice.[77] Therefore, Trautmann has to find some other works as his Control Material.

This leads to two other difficulties about which it will be better to quote Trautmann himself. 'We can never prove the proposition that a given word is always evenly distributed within authors, regardless of context, and other possibly disturbing factors... there must always remain a doubt, however small, that in some author or some text these words may not be evenly distributed. This, however, is the status of any scientific proposition: it has not been disproved in experiment, but the critic can always do so.'[78]

Secondly, '. . . what is a good discriminator on some occasions is poor on another. Color of eyes is a poor discriminator of men: a great number share the same color, just as a fair number must share rates identical or indistinguishable from each other for the use of a certain word.'[79] Trautmann hopes to improve the position by using several discriminators in combination. But he does not seem to have done so in his study of the *Arthaśāstra*, which is based only on a study of *ca* and *vā*. Therefore, he thinks that to solve an authorship problem such as that of the *Arthaśāstra*, some measures of luck and a good deal of careful work is necessary. It seems that luck has eluded him in spite of all the careful work that he may have done.

That the statistical method is not invariably conclusive is also exemplified by Trautmann's treatment of his Control Material and his study of the two samples of Book 7 of the *Arthaśāstra*.[79a]His conclusions about Gaṅgeśa's *Tattvacintāmaṇi* have already been dealt with, but Trautmann also tries to test the authorship by his statistical method in the case of narrative and other works in verse. 'Of the five classical poets, Kālidāsa, Bhāravi, Kumāradāsa, Māgha and Bilhaṇa, suppose their works had come to us anonymously, would we find no significant divergence between the *śloka* type of the two works of Kālidāsa, *Raghuvaṁśa* and *Kumārasambhava* and, if so, would we be able to distinguish the five authors from each other? Table 4.10 shows the answer is 'yes-almost'.'[80] Yet, thereafter Trautmann points out the cases where the test fails. 'The result of the two Kālidāsa works admittedly borders on the 5% level of significance perhaps attributable to changes in style with the passage of time. Between the five authors the *śloka* proves itself an efficient discriminator, except that it fails to distinguish Kālidāsa and Bhāravi from Bilhaṇa.'[81] Again, in the case of Kalhaṇa, Jonarāja and *Mānasollāsa*, 'while the tests easily distinguish *Mānasollāsa* from Kalhaṇa and Jonarāja. . . they fail to distinguish the author of the *Rājataraṅgiṇī* (Kalhaṇa) from its continuator (Jonarāja). Evidently Jonarāja has succeeded in emulating his predecessor's style in this respect'.[82] Thus, while Trautmann admits the failure of his method at some places, he tries to shift the blame somewhere, on the editor in the case of Gaṅgeśa's *Tattvacintāmaṇi*, on the change in style in Kālidasa's two works, on Jonarāja emulating the style of Kalhaṇa, and in the case of two parts of Books 7 of the *Arthaśāstra* as an outrageous event 'which the statistician is bound to meet from time to time'.[83]

4. Trautmann's arguments against Kauṭilya's authorship of *Arthaśāstra*

So far an attempt has been made to show that the difference in the use of *ca* and *vā* is based on context and not authorship and that Trautmann's statistics fails when he deals with either the *Arthaśāstra* (as his Books are not grouped according to his statistics) or his Control Material whether from works in prose or verse. This is so either because the work of one author shows significant difference in its different portions (Kālidāsa, Gaṅgeśa, Somadeva and the two samples of Book 7 of the *Arthaśāstra*) or because the statistics refuse to demonstrate significant difference in the works of two authors (fails to distinguish Kālidāsa and Bhāravi from Bilhaṇa or Kalhaṇa from Jonarāja). It would now be useful to discuss the negative side of Trautmann's argument, i.e. his attempt to prove that Kauṭilya was not the original writer of the *Arthaśāstra* (he might have been an editor).[84] It is for this purpose that it became necessary for Trautmann to deny the originality of the verses and colophons at the end of chapters and the originality of the first and last chapters.

Later additions according to Trautmann

Trautmann's most important argument in support of his theory of later additions is that the division of the work into chapters is a later innovation—'the work of a later, tidying and organizing hand, reworking a text already divided by books and topics, and already possessing an adequate introduction in *Arthaśāstra* 1.2'.[85] That the division into chapters is a later idea enables Trautmann to claim that the verses and colophons at the end of chapters are also later additions, and thus to refute the fact that Kauṭilya is the original writer of the whole work as stated in 1.1.19, 2.10.62, 15.1.72 or that Kauṭilya was the contemporary of Narendra, i.e. Candragupta (2.10.63) or of the Nandas (15.1.72). Not satisfied with this he tries to prove that chapter 1 (a table of contents) and Book 15 (which consists of only one chapter, on devices used in the scientific work) are also later additions because both these not only point towards the unity of the whole treatise, but also refer to Kauṭilya.

(a) Divisions into chapters

It would be advisable to examine first the question of the division into chapters. Trautmann's contention on this point is that the *Arthaśāstra* has a three-fold division—into Books *(adhikaraṇas)*, chapters *(adhyāyās)* and Sections *(prakaraṇas)*, and while each Book and Section deals with a subject, the chapters, he indirectly hints, do not deal with any. 'The scheme of books and topics is quite clear and rational, being based on subject-matter, but it is difficult to see on what principle the division into chapters was made.'[86] So the division into chapters is not only secondary but was introduced later, though he admits Kangle's argument (but not fully) that the division into *prakaraṇas* (sections) is according to subject-matter, whereas the *adhyāyās* (chapters) are approximately of equal length for purposes of study.[87] While opposing Kangle's argument that the chapters have been made somewhat equal for the purpose of study (*adhyayana*), Trautmann points out that neither the Sections, nor the chapters are equal, e.g., three chapters of Topic 1 (2–4) comprise only 35 *sūtras*, whereas one undivided chapter of Topic 30 contains 117 *sūtras*. (This point will be discussed later). Apart from Trautmann's argument, just mentioned, there is another more important reason for considering the division into chapters as a secondary division, viz., the table of contents (1st chapter) gives only the titles of Sections and not of chapters. However, Trautmann does not advance this argument probably because then he would have to accept the first chapter to be a part of the main work as it originally stood. Yet by accepting the veracity of 1.1.18 and of the division of the work into 180 Sections, Trautmann indirectly accepts that the division into chapters is not a later device, because this division is also mentioned in this *sūtra*.

It is true that each Book and Section deals with a subject, but even when a Section (Trautmann calls it a topic probably to show that a chapter does not deal with any topic) is divided into chapters, each chapter relates to a topic or a subject or a number of subjects.[88] In the greater part of the *Arthaśāstra*, i.e. at 93 places, chapters and Sections are common, covering the same topics. At 12 places Sections are divided into chapters. This seems to have been done where it was probably felt that, though the Section itself deals with one subject, it includes a number of topics which should be separately treated as chapters or part-chapters. For example, it may have been thought that Section one on 'Enumeration of the Sciences' (*Vidyasāmuddeśaḥ*), though a very small section, is, as Trautmann says,[89] divided into three parts: (a) Establishing Philosophy *(Ānvīkṣikīsthāpanā)*, (b) Establishing the Vedic Lore *(Trayīsthāpanā)*, and (c) Establishing Economics and the Science of Politics *(Vārttāsthāpanā daṇḍanītisthāpanā ca)*, greater importance having been given to *ānvīkṣikī* and *Trayī*. Or, Section 116, entitled pacts for securing an ally, money, land and an undertaking, is divided into four chapters *mitrasandhi, hiraṇyasandhiśca, bhūmisandhi* (two chapters of which one is for settled and another for unsettled land) and *karmasandhi*.

At 36 places chapters have been divided into Sections because: (1) either some Sections (twenty-two) are so small, consisting of only one to seven *sūtras*,[90] that the writer must have felt that it would not be proper to treat them as chapters, or, (2) parts of them were so closely related to each other that the writer must have felt that it would be useful to place them together, for example, the chapter on procedural law (3.1) which has two Sections—Sec. 57 on determination of (valid and invalid) transactions and Sec. 58 on filing of law-suits, or (3) some of the Sections included within a chapter are so much intertwined that they, as Trautmann himself admits, 'are unmarked and difficult to identify'.[91] It is true the chapters are of unequal length (comprising 9 to 117 *sūtras*), yet they are not so uneven as are the Sections, which have one[92] to 157 *sūtras*[93] with some Sections (mentioned above) consisting of very few *sūtras*. It is here accepted that the division into chapters is a secondary division, in the sense that in the *Arthaśāstra*, Sections are given a greater importance than chapters, for only Sections are mentioned in the Table of Contents, and, therefore, in the headings of chapters also the divisions into Sections are mentioned. Yet it is difficult to accept that the division into chapters is a later device because, as stated above, some of the Sections being very small and some others indiscernible, the writer must have felt that a division into chapters was very necessary, and so whereas the head of each chapter gives the Section numbers, the chapter-wise countings are given in the colophons. Of course, Trautmann considers the colophons also to be a later addition, but if the chapter divisions, as argued above, were necessary because of the lopsidedness of

Sections and were, therefore, not later, the colophons must also have been there from the beginning, for nearly every Sanskrit work has a colophon or a number of colophons.

It is not only in the *Arthaśāstra*, but in other ancient Indian works also there is such a three-fold division, e.g. *Śatapatha Brāhamaṇa* (*khaṇḍa, adhyāya,* and *brahamaṇa*), *Āpastamba Kalpasūtra (praṣna, paṭala, kaṇḍikā)* and *Baudhāyana Kalpasūtra (praṣna, adhyāya, khaṇḍa).* Though it is more difficult to understand the basis of the three-fold division in these works, Kauṭilya's three-fold division is, in comparison, more understandable. What is here emphasized is that an editor was not needed to divide the *Arthaśāstra* into *adhikaraṇas, prakaraṇas* and *adhyāyas;* the original writer could have done that for reasons stated above.

It would be interesting to observe that the twelve Sections that have been divided into chapters are in Books 1 and 2, Book 3, Books 7, 12 and 14, though according to Trautmann, Books 2, 3, 7 and 12 have different authors. Similarly, the 36 chapters that are divided into Sections are in Books 1 to 3, 5, 7 to 13; authored by four different persons, according to Trautmann. This is another ground for holding that the division both into Sections and chapters is original, though the latter division may be secondary.

(b) Chapter 1

Trautmann has other grounds for considering chapter 1 of the *Arthaśāstra* to be a later addition. He makes two statements: firstly, that the first chapter of the *Arthaśāstra* is unique in that it contains no topic (Section). Secondly, that 'in the text itself there are the right number of topics 180, without considering Chapter 1.1 to contain a topic', which means that this chapter is not within the bounds of *Arthaśāstra*. The first statement is correct, but the reason, as Kangle says,[94] for not considering it to be a section, is that it gives a Table of Contents and does not deal with any topic of the subject proper. The second statement is wrong. *Sūtra* 1.1.18 which speaks of 180 sections in the *Arthaśāstra,* which are to be found, excluding Chapter 1.1, also contains another fact, i.e. that there are 150 chapters in that work. Though this chapter is excluded from 180 sections mentioned in the *sūtra,* it is not excluded from 150 chapters spoken of therein. Trautmann refrains even from referring to the fact that the *Arthaśāstra* contains 150 chapters, because that would be a reason for demolishing his contention about the first chapter, and that of the division into chapters as being a later addition, for if he accepts the division into Sections mentioned in 1.1.18 as an original division he would also have to accept, on that very ground, that the division into chapters is also original. Not only that, the fact that Trautmann puts forward the argument that 180 sections are mentioned in chapter 1, he also indirectly accepts the originality of chapter 1. Lastly, if Trautmann's argument that the terminal verses are later additions is accepted then his statement that there are the right number of topics, i.e. 180, in the *Arthaśāstra,* is proved wrong, because one whole Section (102) in Book 7, chapter 3 is wholly in the form of verses (which may be termed terminal verses) and so the number of sections remain 179 and not 180.

(c) Book 15

Trautmann also considers Book 14, i.e. *Tantrayukti,* to be a later addition[95] and the only reason given for that is that it refers to the first chapter (15.1.4). However, the first chapter is not a later addition, as is clear from the fact that the Table of Contents of that chapter contains no chapter-headings, but only section-headings which are considered by Trautmann to be primary divisions, as is clear from the fact that though it is not one of the 180 sections for the reason given above, but is otherwise one of the 150 chapters mentioned in 1.1.18; and that even 1.1.18–19 (a *sūtra* and a *śloka*), which Kangle considers to be later additon,[96] though they are not found in one Malayalam commentary, do not appear to be an interpolation as they are found in all other available manuscripts (cf. pp. 11–12 above)

(d) Terminal verses

Lastly, Trautmann considered all the terminal verses and colophons as later additions, and this he took to be an added argument to his contention that the division of the *Arthaśāstra* into chapters was a later change. This appeared to him to support his position probably because it is in these verses that Kauṭilya is mentioned as the author of the *Arthaśāstra*. For his contention that the colophons are later introductions, Trautmann has no other argument except that they are found at the end of chapters, which, according to him, is not only a secondary, but is also a later change; he advances another argument for maintaining that the verses are later additions. 'The occasional usefulness of the verses to the argument of the prose, or occasional continuity with the prose scarcely weighs against their usual lack of utility and continuity.'[97] To support the contention that the terminal verses were added later, he quotes Renou (p. 75) to show that if the division into chapters had been made later, the terminal verses should also be a later addition. However, Renou adds, 'Nevertheless certain compact group of verses have their *utility* in perfecting a doctrine; and what is more telling, there are several signs indicating that there is continuity in sense between the prose and the verse' (quoted from Trautmann). It would seem from this that, according to Renou, the argument of Trautmann's considering the terminal verses as later additions does not have enough validity. Yet Trautmann agrees with Renou that 'the question cannot be resolved without nuances', but Trautmann does not go into nuances. Now, the decision about the utility of something is a subjective matter. Some *ślokas* which are considered by one scholar as having no utility can be thought of as quite useful by another scholar. So the matter of utility can be taken up later. The continuity in sense of verses with the previous prose portion may be dealt with here. On examining through all the chapters of the *Arthaśāstra* it was found: (i) that it is only in a very few chapters of it that there is a lack of continuity. They are 2.4, 34; 3.3 (these verses should be placed in 3.2), 10, 13, 14; 5.3; 8.1; and 9.4 (nine in all). (ii) In addition in some cases the continuity of final verses with the previous prose portion may be considered doubtful by some scholars—1.7 (though it is an introduction to the next chapter); 2.1, 25; 3.12, 17; 5.2; 7.9; 9.3 and 10.6 (nine in all). (iii) In a few chapters a few verses are out of context, four verses out of seven in 1.19 (even these verses, i.e. the last four are not out of context and are connected with 1.19.1–5); one out of three verses in 4.7; two out of eight in 7.6 (these should have been in 10.3); and two verses out of eight in 7.13. In addition to these chapters, there are a few more, where, though there is continuity between verses at the end and the subject discussed in the previous prose portion,they may be considered additions for reasons other than lack of continuity. (iv) Some of the verses are introduced by some words and it is possible that they are quotations. They are 1.8, 15; 2.18; 4.2; 7.3, 5, and 9.3 (seven in all). (v) Again, in some chapters the final verses come after *iti* at the end. They are 1.4, 6; 2.10, 11, 17, 20; 7.17; 8.3, 5; 12.3; 13.1, 5; 15.1 (thirteen in all). However, in the last mentioned case, i.e. in the verses coming after *iti*, in chapters (1.4, 6; 7.17; 8.3; 12.3) the word *'iti'* does not indicate the end of the subject. (vi) Finally, it seems the writer has closed a subject, probably a *prakaraṇa*, and thereafter follow verses, though they are more or less connected with the subject discussed earlier, (2.4, 29, 30; 3.3, 10, 12, 13; 5.3; 7.12, 13,17; 8.4)[98] Thus only (i) in nine chapters that there is certainly a lack of continuity between the preceeding prose and the terminal verses; (ii) in nine other chapters it is a matter of doubt, and the benefit of doubt must go to the author, (iii) in four chapters the verses continue the preceding subject, but a few verses at the end are not connected, though in one chapter, as said above, even these are connected with the *sūtras* at the very beginning of that very chapter. (iii) In twenty-four other chapters the terminal verses can be considered later additions for other reasons though they continue the same subject (categories iv, v and four chapters mentioned in vi-2.29, 30; 7.12; 8.4) Apart from these 46 chapters, in 102 chapters out of 148 (the first and last chapters having been considered later additions by Trautmann) the verses at the end do not show any reason why they could have been considered as having been added later. Even in the 46 chapters referred to here in 24 chapters it may be considered doubtful, whether the original writer has placed them here (even though they may be quotations taken from somewhere by the original writer).[99] Considering all these details it is difficult to accept Trautmann's contention that there is usual lack of continuity between the prose portion and the final verses as also his conclusion thereon that the verses are later additions.

With respect of the utility of the terminal verses all of them seemd to be useful in the sense that something is said there, which is a little different from, though connected with, what is found earlier in the chapter. However, there is one other fact indicating the utility of these verses. As there is in about two thirds of the chapters only one verse at the end, therefore, this verse seems to have been placed there to signify the end of the chapter, particularly because in many chapters the sub-topic that is found in the prose portion immediately before that verse is continued in this terminal verse itself, and the writer could have put the idea contained in the vese even in a prose *sūtra* e.g. I.2.10-12; I.13.22-26; I.18.13-16; etc. upto XIV.2.45 (connected with the whole of the previous prose portion). Even if the verse is not so connected with the previous prose it is yet useful it could have been in prose, but still the verse is there for no other reason than indicating the completion of the chapter.

The foregoing discussion tries to show that the difference in the use of *ca* and *vā* in different Books (as also in different chapters of Books or in different parts of some chapters) is due to difference of context and not to difference in authorship. It also shows that Kauṭilya is indeed the author of the entire work known as *Arthaśāstra*, including the first and the last chapter and terminal verses and colophons, and it was he who divided the work into chapters, and Trautmann's claim about later additions is not tenable.

Even if the major part of the scholarly world accepts the arguments advanced above, the debate, as Trautmann says in p. 7 of his book, will continue. Let us hope some other day, some other Basham will arise, and he will inspire some other Trautmann to try to prove by some other method that the *Arthaśāstra* in its present form was written in the third century AD.

Table VII

In this table are to be found zero, one, two, three and three plus and the total occurrences of *vā* and *ca* per chapter, per 300 sentence-sample, and per Book. This can enable the reader to check the figures given in the preceeding discussion. These figures have been manually gathered from the *Arthaśāstra* and, in spite of all the care taken that they are correct, mistakes may have crept in.

Book 1

		Occurrences of *vā*						Occurrences of *ca*					
Chapter	Sūtras	0	1	2	3	3+	Total	0	1	2	3	3+	Total
2	(11)	11	0	0	0	0	0	6	4	0	1	0	7
3	(15)	14	1	0	0	0	1	3	11	1	0	0	13
4	(15)	14	1	0	0	0	1	12	3	0	0	0	3
5	(16)	16	0	0	0	0	0	7	8	1	0	0	10
6	(10)	9	1	0	0	0	1	4	6	0	0	0	6
7	(8)	6	1	1	0	0	3	6	1	1	0	0	3
8	(29)	28	1	0	0	0	1	27	2	0	0	0	2
9	(10)	10	0	0	0	0	0	6	2	1	0	1(8)	12
10	(15)	12	2	1	0	0	4	13	2	0	0	0	2
11	(21)	18	2	1	0	0	4	9	9	3	0	0	15
12	(18)	13	4	1	0	0	6	12	6	0	0	0	6
13	(25)	20	4	0	1	0	7	17	7	1	0	0	9
14	(10)	9	0	0	1	0	3	8	2	0	0	0	2
15	(58)	50	7	1	0	0	9	47	11	0	0	0	11
16	(32)	26	5	0	0	1(10)	15	23	7	2	0	0	11
17	(7)	7	0	0	0	0	0	5	1	1	0	0	3
	(300)	263	29	5	2	1(10)	55	205	82	11	1	1(8)	115

Chapter	Sūtras	0	1	2	3	3+	Total	0	1	2	3	3+	Total
17	(44)	40	3	1	0	0	5	37	5	2	0	0	9
18	(15)	7	7	1	0	0	9	10	4	1	0	0	6
19	(29)	24	5	0	0	0	5	16	13	0	0	0	13
20	(21)	16	4	0	0	1(4)	8	14	5	2	0	0	9
21	(28)	25	3	0	0	0	3	12	10	5	0	1(10)	30
	(137)	112	22	2	0	1(4)	30	89	37	10	0	1(10)	67
Total	(437)	375	51	7	2	1(4) 1(10)	85	294	119	21	1	1(8) 1(10)	182

Note: (Book 1) : In the above table the figures given are for no (zero) occurrence or one occurrence or two occurrences or three occurrences, or more than three occurrence of *vā* in a sentence (*Sūtra)* on the left hand side and for *ca* on the right hand side. The'300 sentence sample ends with the 7th *sūtra* of chapter 17. These figures are totalled up. Other 44 *sūtras* of chapter 17 and the other four remaining chapters are accounted for below. They contain 137 *sūtras*. Their total is given thereafter. The grand total of 437 *sūtras* is found at the end. This method is followed in other Books also.

In four chapters of Book 1, as against the rest, the number of *vā-s* is more than *ca-s* (chapters 10, 14, 16, 18) but the difference was not so much as would have needed a separate mention, the greatest difference being in chapter 16 (15 *vā-s* and 11 *ca-s*) and chapter 18 (9 *vā-s* and 6 *ca-s*). The difference in chapter 16 is because of one *sūtra* (No. 29) which has 10 *vā-s*, though its subject is not of a different type, while chapter 18 has been dealt with earlier (pp. 85, 88, 97, 98–9).

Book 2

		Occurrences of *vā*						Occurrences of *ca*					
Chapter	Sūtras	0	1	2	3	3+	Total	0	1	2	3	3+	Total
1	(35)	27	7	1	0	0	9	23	10	2	0	0	14
2	(14)	12	2	0	0	0	2	9	4	1	0	0	6
3	(33)	20	10	0	1	2(4)	21	25	8	0	0	0	8
4	(31)	29	2	0	0	0	2	19	10	2	0	0	14
5	(21)	19	2	0	0	0	2	14	6	0	1	0	9
6	(27)	26	1	0	0	0	1	12	12	3	0	0	18
7	(40)	34	5	1	0	0	7	25	14	1	0	0	16
8	(31)	25	5	0	0	1(4)	9	24	6	1	0	0	8
9	(31)	29	2	0	0	0	2	20	11	0	0	0	11
10	(37)	37	0	0	0	0	0	33	4	0	0	0	4
	(300)	258	36	2	1	3(4)	55	204	85	10	1	0	108
10	(13)	13	0	0	0	0	0	11	2	0	0	0	2
11	(115)	95	20	0	0	0	20	80	32	3	0	0	38
12	(33)	22	7	3	1	0	16	17	13	2	1	0	20
13	(59)	48	10	1	0	0	12	37	20	2	0	0	24
14	(54)	32	18	4	0	0	26	41	12	1	0	0	14
15	(26)	25	0	1	0	0	2	16	10	0	0	0	10
	(300)	235	55	9	1	0	76	202	89	8	1	0	108

Chapter	Sūtras	0	1	2	3	3+	Total	0	1	2	3	3+	Total
15	(37)	32	5	0	0	0	5	28	8	1	0	0	10
16	(24)	17	7	0	0	0	7	13	11	0	0	0	11
17	(16)	15	1	0	0	0	1	12	3	1	0	0	5
18	(20)	20	0	0	0	0	0	10	9	0	1	0	12
19	(45)	39	5	1	0	0	7	41	3	1	0	0	5
20	(64)	61	3	0	0	0	3	51	12	0	1	0	15
21	(30)	22	6	2	0	0	10	19	9	2	0	0	13
22	(14)	11	3	0	0	0	3	8	6	0	0	0	6
23	(18)	15	3	0	0	0	3	6	8	4	0	0	16
24	(27)	21	5	1	0	0	7	16	5	4	2	0	19
25	(5)	2	1	1	1	0	6	4	0	1	0	0	2
	(300)	255	39	5	1	0	52	208	74	14	4	0	114
25	(34)	25	7	2	0	0	11	21	9	3	1	0	18
26	(13)	11	1	1	0	0	3	8	5	0	0	0	5
27	(29)	19	8	2	0	0	12	22	5	2	0	0	9
28	(26)	21	3	2	0	0	7	14	9	1	2	0	17
29	(47)	42	4	1	0	0	6	34	8	4	0	1(6)	22
30	(49)	40	8	0	0	1(4)	12	29	20	0	0	0	20
31	(17)	15	1	1	0	0	3	13	4	0	0	0	4
32	(20)	20	0	0	0	0	0	11	9	0	0	0	9
33	(10)	10	0	0	0	0	0	6	2	1	0	1(4)	8
34	(11)	8	2	1	0	0	4	8	3	0	0	0	3
35	(14)	13	1	0	0	0	1	2	7	3	1	1(4)	20
36	(30)	27	3	0	0	0	3	19	8	3	0	0	14
	(300)	251	38	10	0	1(4)	62	187	89	17	4	2(4) 1(6)	149

. . .contd.

Chapter	Sūtras	0	1	2	3	3+	Total	0	1	2	3	3+	Total
36	(15)	14	1	0	0	0	1	5	10	0	0	0	10
Total	1215	1013	169	26	3	4(4)	246	806	347	49	10	2(4)	489

Note: (Book 2) : There are four samples of 300 sentences each. The total of 0, 1, 2, 3, and more than 3 occurrences of *vā* and *ca* and of their total occurrences can be found at the end of each sample. The total of the rest of the 15 sentences and the grand total of Book 2 is given at the end.

In Book 2 while there are generally more *ca-s* and less *vā-s.* In chapters 3 and 14 there are significantly more *vā-s* than *ca-s.* Chapter 3 has been spoken of on pp. 84, 87, 90, 92, 94 and chapter 14 is an exception. In chapters 8, 19, 27 and 34, too there are more *vā-s* but there are minor differences. Chapter 25 also has no major differences in figures of *vā* and *ca*, yet it can be treated as an exception. Exception means that, either the subject being theoretical or less political there are more *vā-s* whereas there should have been more *ca-s*, or the subject being political there are more *ca-s* instead of more *vā-s*. Such chapters are 10 out of 48 (see p. 91 above).

Book 3

		Occurrences of *vā*						Occurrences of *ca*					
Chapter	Sūtras	0	1	2	3	3+	Total	0	1	2	3	3+	Total
1	(37)	31	6	0	0	0	6	26	10	0	1	0	13
2	(47)	36	11	0	0	0	11	38	7	2	0	0	11
3	(31)	22	9	0	0	0	9	25	6	0	0	0	6
4	(41)	31	8	2	0	0	12	37	4	0	0	0	4
5	(32)	26	5	1	0	0	7	24	6	2	0	0	10
6	(23)	17	6	0	0	0	6	20	2	0	1	0	5
7	(39)	34	5	0	0	0	5	34	5	0	0	0	5
8	(27)	18	5	4	0	0	13	21	5	1	0	0	7
9	(23)	16	4	3	0	0	10	20	3	0	0	0	3
	(300)	231	59	10	0	0	79	245	48	5	2	0	64
9	(14)	13	1	0	0	0	1	11	3	0	0	0	3
10	(45)	35	8	2	0	0	12	36	7	2	0	0	11
11	(49)	31	14	4	0	0	22	40	8	1	0	0	10
12	(52)	30	16	5	0	1(5)	31	35	15	1	1	0	20
13	(36)	25	10	1	0	0	12	26	9	1	0	0	11
14	(36)	26	7	3	0	0	13	28	7	1	0	0	9
15	(18)	15	3	0	0	0	3	13	5	0	0	0	5
16	(41)	29	11	1	0	0	13	28	11	2	0	0	15
17	(9)	9	0	0	0	0	0	8	1	0	0	0	1
	(300)	213	70	16	0	1(5)	107	225	66	8	1	0	85

. . .contd.

Chapter	Sūtras	0	1	2	3	3+	Total	0	1	2	3	3+	Total
17	(5)	3	1	1	0	0	3	4	1	0	0	0	1
18	(11)	10	1	0	0	0	1	6	4	1	0	0	6
19	(29)	24	4	1	0	0	6	22	5	1	0	1(6)	13
20	(23)	20	1	2	0	0	5	12	10	1	0	0	12
	(68)	57	7	4	0	0	15	44	20	3	0	1(6)	32
	(668)	501	136	30	0	1(5)	201	514	134	16	3	1(6)	181

Note: (Book 3): In this Book chapters 1 and 17-20 with their subject procedural law and Criminal law have, as against the general trend, more *ca-s* than *vā-s*. Though the differences between *vā* and *ca*, are minor, in different chapters as a whole the two groups have been differentiated.

Book 4

Chapter	Sūtras	Occurrences of *vā* 0	1	2	3	3+	Total	Occurrences of *ca* 0	1	2	3	3+	Total
1	(64)	61	3	0	0	0	3	50	13	1	0	0	15
2	(35)	28	5	2	0	0	9	30	5	0	0	0	5
3	(43)	28	11	3	1	0	20	30	13	0	0	0	13
4	(22)	17	3	1	1	0	8	15	7	0	0	0	7
5	(17)	11	6	0	0	0	6	13	4	0	0	0	4
6	(19)	11	4	2	1	1(6)	17	14	3	2	0	0	7
7	(22)	13	4	4	1	0	15	21	1	0	0	0	1
8	(28)	22	5	0	1	0	8	17	9	2	0	0	13
9	(27)	9	13	4	0	1(7)	28	22	4	1	0	0	6
10	(16)	4	6	3	2	1(4)	22	10	4	2	0	0	8
11	(7)	6	1	0	0	0	1	6	1	0	0	0	1
	(300)	210	61	19	7	1(6), 1(7), 1(4)	137	228	64	8	0	0	80

		Occurrences of *vā*						Occurrences of *ca*					
Chapter	Sūtras	0	1	2	3	3+	Total	0	1	2	3	3+	Total
11	(18)	14	3	1	0	0	5	13	5	0	0	0	5
12	(37)	30	5	2	0	0	9	23	14	0	0	0	14
13	(40)	26	12	2	0	0	16	29	8	2	1	0	15
	(95)	70	20	5	0	0	30	65	27	2	1	0	34
	(395)	280	81	24	7	1(6), 1(7), 1(4)	167	293	91	10	1	0	114

Note: (Book 4): In this Book, chapters 1, 8 and 12 are exceptions (see p. 91 above).

Book 5

		Occurrences of *vā*						Occurrences of *ca*					
Chapter	Sūtras	0	1	2	3	3+	Total	0	1	2	3	3+	Total
1	(56)	29	17	4	4	1(5), 1(7)	49	53	3	0	0	0	3
2	(69)	41	20	5	3	0	39	50	17	2	0	0	21
3	(46)	40	6	0	0	0	6	26	19	1	0	0	21
4	(10)	8	2	0	0	0	2	5	1	2	1	1(4)	12
5	(14)	11	3	0	0	0	3	6	7	1	0	0	9
6	(43)	22	18	3	0	0	24	27	16	1	0	0	18
	(238)	151	66	12	7	1(5), 1(7)	123	167	63	7	1	1(4)	84

Book 6

Chapter	Sūtras	Occurrences of *vā* 0	1	2	3	3+	Total	Occurrences of *ca* 0	1	2	3	3+	Total
1	(14)	13	1	0	0	0	1	11	2	0	1	0	5
2	(38)	32	3	2	0	1(7)	14	32	5	1	0	0	7
	(52)	45	4	2	0	1(7)	15	43	7	1	1	0	12

Book 7

Chapter	Sūtras	Occurrences of *vā* 0	1	2	3	3+	Total	Occurrences of *ca* 0	1	2	3	3+	Total
1	(37)	22	10	2	0	1(4), 1(6), 1(13)	37	34	3	0	0	0	3
2	(24)	12	8	2	1	1(5)	20	23	0	1	0	0	2
3	(20)	15	4	1	0	0	6	18	2	0	0	0	2
4	(21)	12	4	2	1	1(4), 1(9)	24	16	3	1	1	0	8
5	(35)	18	16	1	0	0	18	29	4	2	0	0	8
6	(32)	24	4	3	1	0	13	24	6	2	0	0	10
7	(30)	15	5	4	3	2(4), 1(5)	35	30	0	0	0	0	0
8	(33)	21	7	4	1	0	18	25	4	3	1	0	13
9	(40)	29	11	0	0	0	11	34	4	2	0	0	8
10	(28)	21	7	0	0	0	7	19	7	1	1	0	12
	(300)	189	76	19	7	4(4) 2(5), 1(6), 1(9), 1(13)	189	252	33	12	3	0	66

Chapter	Sūtras	0	1	2	3	3+	Total	0	1	2	3	3+	Total
10	(9)	9	0	0	0	0	0	4	3	2	0	0	7
11	(44)	36	7	0	1	0	10	36	5	2	1	0	12
12	(28)	24	3	1	0	0	5	20	7	1	0	0	9
13	(34)	31	3	0	0	0	3	26	8	0	0	0	8
14	(28)	18	5	4	1	0	16	22	4	2	0	0	8
15	(29)	17	11	0	0	1(18)	29	23	5	1	0	0	7
16	(32)	26	5	1	0	0	7	19	10	3	0	0	16
17	(60)	35	18	7	0	0	32	53	7	0	0	0	7
18	(30)	16	11	1	0	1(4), 1(6)	23	25	3	2	0	0	7
	(294)	212	63	14	2	1(4), 1(6), 1(18)	125	228	52	13	1	0	81
Total	(594)	401	139	33	9	5(4), 2(5), 2(6), 1(9), 1(13), 1(18)	314	480	ε5	25	4	0	147

Note: (Book 7): In this Book also, although in chapters 10 to 13 differences in *vā* and *ca* are minor, as they form a single category together with chapter 9, they have been put together. Chapter 9 is an exception.

Book 8

Chapter	Sūtras	Occurrences of *vā* 0	1	2	3	3+	Total	Occurrences of *ca* 0	1	2	3	3+	Total
1	(60)	53	7	0	0	0	7	32	24	3	1	0	33
2	(25)	17	5	3	0	0	11	20	5	0	0	0	5
3	(64)	60	2	2	0	0	6	41	19	3	1	0	28
4	(49)	41	8	0	0	0	8	37	9	1	2	0	17
5	(18)	17	1	0	0	0	1	18	0	0	0	0	0
	(216)	188	23	5	0	0	33	148	57	7	4	0	83

Note: Book 8 is less political or theoretical in the sense that it does not deal with political and counter moves but with calamities which afflict the elements of the state. Chapter 2 is an exception.

Book 9

Chapter	Sūtras	Occurrences of *vā* 0	1	2	3	3+	Total	Occurrences of *ca* 0	1	2	3	3+	Total
1	(51)	46	4	1	0	0	6	37	7	4	2	1(4)	25
2	(29)	19	4	1	1	2(4), 1(5), 1(6)	28	16	12	1	0	0	14
3	(41)	19	17	3	1	1(7)	33	34	4	1	2	0	12
4	(25)	23	1	0	0	1(7)	8	21	4	0	0	0	4
5	(31)	17	13	1	0	0	15	27	2	2	0	0	6
6	(72)	49	15	7	1	0	32	61	9	2	0	0	13
7	(51)	43	6	1	1	0	11	48	3	0	0	0	3
	(300)	216	60	14	4	2(4), 1(5), 1(6), 2(7)	133	244	41	10	4	1(4)	77

Chapter	Sūtras	0	1	2	3	3+	Total	0	1	2	3	3+	Total
7	(32)	27	3	1	1	0	8	27	4	1	0	0	6
Total	(332)	243	63	15	5	2(4), 1(5), 1(6), 2(7),	141	271	45	11	4	1(4)	83

Note: Chapter 1 of this book is spoken of above at pp. 83–4, 89 and 93, 95–9.

Book 10

		Occurrences of *vā*						Occurrences of *ca*					
Chapter	Sūtras	0	1	2	3	3+	Total	0	1	2	3	3+	Total
1	(16)	15	0	1	0	0	2	6	9	1	0	0	11
2	(19)	14	2	1	0	1(4), 1(5)	13	13	6	0	0	0	6
3	(54)	37	16	1	0	0	18	41	11	2	0	0	15
4	(17)	16	1	0	0	0	1	7	8	0	1	1(4)	15
5	(56)	43	13	0	0	0	13	49	5	2	0	0	9
6	(47)	43	4	0	0	0	4	42	5	0	0	0	5
	(209)	168	36	3	0	1(4), 1(5)	51	158	44	5	1	1(4)	61

Note : A discussion about chapter 1 and 4 is to be found on pp. 89–90, 93, 96.

Book 11

		Occurrences of *vā*						Occurrences of *ca*					
Chapter	Sūtras	0	1	2	3	3+	Total	0	1	2	3	3+	Total
1	(55)	31	17	5	2	0	33	43	11	1	0	0	13

Book 12

		Occurrences of *vā*						Occurrences of *ca*					
Chapter	Sūtras	0	1	2	3	3+	Total	0	1	2	3	3+	Total
1	(31)	19	10	2	0	0	14	28	3	0	0	0	3
2	(32)	19	13	0	0	0	13	16	12	3	0	1(4)	22
3	(20)	14	3	2	1	0	10	12	4	1	3	0	15
4	(28)	4	14	9	1	0	35	24	4	0	0	0	4
5	(50)	16	25	5	3	1(11)	55	42	7	1	0	0	9
	(161)	72	65	18	5	1(11)	127	122	30	5	3	1(4)	53

Note : Chapters 2 and 3 are exceptions.

Book 13

Chapter	Sūtras	Occurrences of *vā* 0	1	2	3	3+	Total	Occurrences of *ca* 0	1	2	3	3+	Total
1	(20)	19	0	0	1	0	3	6	12	2	0	0	16
2	(44)	21	17	4	2	0	31	36	6	2	0	0	10
3	(57)	24	29	3	1	0	38	50	5	2	0	0	9
4	(61)	32	22	5	2	0	38	47	10	4	0	0	18
5	(23)	18	3	2	0	0	7	6	12	3	2	0	24
	(205)	114	71	14	6	0	117	145	45	13	2	0	77

Note: Chapter 1 is an exception, while chapter 5 is dealt with on pp. 90, 93, 96.

Book 14

Chapter	Sūtras	Occurrences of *vā* 0	1	2	3	3+	Total	Occurrences of *ca* 0	1	2	3	3+	Total
1	(35)	23	9	3	0	0	15	25	7	3	0	0	13
2	(40)	29	8	2	1	0	15	38	2	0	0	0	2
3	(62)	53	7	1	1	0	12	53	9	0	0	0	9
4	(12)	11	1	0	0	0	1	10	2	0	0	0	2
	(149)	116	25	6	2	0	43	126	20	3	0	0	26

References

[1] M. Winternitz, *History of Indian Literature*, tr. Subhadra Jha, vol. III, part 2, Delhi, 1977, p. 589.
[2] *Geschichte der Indischen Literature*, 1920. Translation referred to in ref. no.1, pp. 588–96.
[3] *Arthaśāstra of Kauṭilya*, Introduction, Lahore, 1923.
[4] *History of Sanskrit Literature*, Oxford University Press, 1920, pp. 458–62.
[5] *Megasthenes und Kauṭilya*, Wien, 1921.
[6] *The Wonder That Was India*, Fontana, 1967, p. 80;
[6a] R.P. Kangle, *The Kauṭilīya Arthaśāstra: A Study*, part III, Bombay, 1965, p. 59.
[7] Thomas R. Trautmann, *Kauṭilya and the Arthaśāstra*, Preface, Leiden, 1971, p. 9.
[8] *Kauṭilya and the Arthaśāstra*, p. 7.
[9] Ibid., p. 10.
[10] Ibid., p. 95.
[11] Ibid., p. 105.
[12] Ibid., p. 117.
[13] Ibid., p. 82.
[14] Ibid., p. 78–80.
[15] See pp. 82–103.
[16] *Kauṭilya and the Arthaśāstra*, op. cit., p. 83.
[16a] Ibid. For these tables, see pp. 92–100 below.
[17] Ibid., p. 100.
[18] In these mentioned chapters, whereas in one part of the chapter there are greater occurrences of *vā*, in the other part there are greater occurrences of *ca*.
[19] *Kauṭilya and the Arthaśāstra*, op. cit., p. 103, Table 4.6.
[20] Ibid., p. 126.
[21] Ibid., p. 126, note 2.
[21a] Ibid., p. 116.
[22] Appendix 9, table 6, pp. 210–11.
[23] *Kauṭilya and the Arthaśāstra*, op. cit., p. 100.
[24] Ibid., see above pp. 77–80; tables 5 and 6 given here on pp. 98–103.
[25] Ibid., p. 114, also p. 91.
[26] Ibid., p. 116.
[27] Ibid., pp. 85–88.
[28] R.P. Kangle, *Kauṭilīya Arthaśāstra*, volume I, Bombay, 1970, 6.2.38.
[29] Figures given by Trautmann, pp. 83–87, table 3.1. to 3.7. The figures given here p. 12 at the end, in table 7 (55 *vā-s* and 108 *ca-s* for Book 2,

sample 1; and 76 *vā-s* and 108 *ca-s* for Book 2, sample 2) differ from those mentioned by Trautmann, in table 3.2, p. 83 (54 *vā-s* and 102 *ca-s* for Book 2, sample 1; and 73 *vā-s* and 111 *ca-s* for Book 2, sample 2), differ from those given by Trautmann but only a little and the mistake can be on either side.

30 *Kauṭilya and the Arthaśāstra*, op. cit., p. 89.

31 Ibid., p. 118.

32 Ibid., pp. 115–17.

33 Ibid., p. 116.

34 Table 3.1.

35 *Sūtras* 1–14.

36 *Sūtras* 15–25.

37 *Kauṭilīya Arthaśāstra*, op. cit., 1.20.1–13, construction of a palace, and, 2.3, construction of a fort.

38 Those chapters, where there are a minor differences in the use of *ca* and *vā*, have been ignored, ten in all; they are, Book 1 (14), Book 2 (8, 19, 25, 27, 34), Book 3 (5, 15, 16), Book 8 (5), Book 14 (4). Five chapters in Book 1 (7, 12), Book 3 (2,7) and Book 4 (11), have an equal number of *ca-s* and *vā-s*. Also see notes given below the *ca* and *vā* figures of these Books, in Table 7.

39 Book 1 (182 *ca-s* and 85 *vā-s*); Book 2 (489 *ca-s* and 246 *vā-s*); Book 8 (83 *ca-s* and 33 *vā-s*).

40 Book 5 (83 *ca-s* and 123 *vā-s*, in all); Book 7 (147 *ca-s* and 314 *vā-s*); Book 9 (83 *ca-s* and 141 *vā-s*); Book 11 (13 *ca-s* and 33 *vā-s*); Book 12 (53 *ca-s* and 127 *vā-s*), Book 13 (77 *ca-s* and 117 *vā-s*), with Book 14 going with this group (26 *ca-s* and 43 *vā-s*).

41 Book 3 (181 *ca-s* and 201 *vā-s*), Book 4 (114 *ca-s* and 167 *vā-s*), Book 6 (15 *vā-s* and 12 *ca-s*), and Book 10 (61 *ca-s* and 51 *vā-s*) can also be placed in this category.

42 *Kauṭilya and the Arthuśāstra*, op. cit., p. 119.

43 Ibid., p. 119.

44 Ibid., p. 119–20.

45 Ibid., p. 118.

46 Ibid., p. 118.

47 Ibid., pp. 118–19.

48 Ibid., p. 121.

49 Ibid., p. 122.

50 Ibid., pp. 119–21.

51 Ibid., pp. 120–21.

52 Ibid., pp. 119–22.

53 Ibid., p. 102–3, see above pp. 77–81.

54 Ibid., p. 120, Table 4.16.

55 Ibid., p. 119.

[56] Ibid., p. 131, table 5.8.
[57] Ibid., pp. 102, 124–5.
[58] Ibid., p. 103, table 4.6.
[59] Ibid., p. 125, table 5.4.
[60] Ibid., p. 125.
[61] Ibid., pp. 123–4, table 5.1.
[62] Ibid., p. 124, table 5.2.
[63] Ibid., p. 129, table 5.6.
[64] Ibid., p. 125.
[65] E.g. 4.3.4. refers to *Niśāntapraṇidhi* (1.20) and to *Nāgarikapraṇidhi* (2.36). Or, 5.1.3 refers to *Gūḍhapuruṣapraṇidhi* (1.12) and *Kṛtyapakṣopagraha* (1.13). Similarly, 5.4.1–5 refers to *ātmasampat* (6.1.6).
[66] E.g. 3.1.1. refers to *saṁgrahaṇa* etc. (2.1.4) and 4.3.8 refers to *madanarasa* (14. 1.16–17).
[67] Books 1 and 2.
[68] *Kauṭilya and the Arthaśāstra,* op. cit., p. 184.
[69] Books 3, 4 and 5.
[70] *Kauṭilya and the Arthaśāstra,* op. cit., pp. 184–5.
[71] Cf. *Kāmandakīyā Nītisāra*, 8.20–41.
[72] *Kauṭilya and the Arthaśāstra,* op. cit., p. 77.
[73] Ibid., p. 174.
[74] Ibid., p. 77.
[75] 1.2.10.
[76] *Kauṭilya and the Arthaśāstra,* op. cit., p. 77.
[77] Ibid., pp. 168, 173–4.
[78] Ibid., p. 92.
[79] Ibid.
[79a] See above, pp. 108–9, 82.
[80] *Kauṭilya and the Arthaśāstra,* op. cit., p. 111.
[81] Ibid., p. 111.
[82] Ibid., p. 113.
[83] Ibid., p. 116.
[84] Ibid., p. 77.
[85] Ibid., p. 75.
[86] Ibid., p. 71.
[87] *Kauṭilya Arthaśāstra: A Study,* part III, p. 25.
[88] There are six such chapters which have a number of subjects, i.e., 1.4; 3.2, 3, 4, 9; 7.9.
[89] *Kauṭilya and the Arthaśāstra,* op. cit., p. 72.
[90] Sections 15, 49, 50, 51, 52, 104, 106, 107, 110, 111, 114, 125, 131, 132, 139, 149, 154, 157, 159, 165, 167, 169.
[91] *Kauṭilya and the Arthaśāstra,* op. cit., p. 71. These are chapter 5.6-sections 94–5; chapter 7.6 - section 111–12; chapter 7.15 - sections 119–20;

chapter 12.3 - section 164–5; chapter 12.4 - section 166–67; chapter 12.5 - section 168–70.

[92] Sections 104, 106, 131, 132, 167, 169.

[93] Section 116.

[94] *Kauṭilya Arthaśāstra: A Study,* part III, p. 25.

[95] *Kauṭilya and the Arthaśāstra,* op. cit., p. 75.

[96] *Kauṭilya Arthaśāstra: A Study,* part III, p. 21.

[97] *Kauṭilīya and the Arthaśāstra,* op. cit., p. 75.

[98] Out of these 12 chapters, eight appear in earlier categories (i.e., 1 to 5). These are 2.4; 3.3, 10, 12, 13, 5.3; 7.13. 17.

[99] In the internal verses found in twelve chapters (1.8, 15. 2.10, 12, 24; 7.5, 6, 9; 13.4; 14.1, 2, 3) belonging to different books which Trautmann considers as authored by different persons, nearly all the above varieties are found (i.e., not properly connected with the previous *sūtras* e.g. 1.8.9, or starting with *iti,* e.g. 2.24.9–10 or introduced by certain words e.g. 7.9.38–49).

Index